PERFORMANCE REVIEW IN LOCAL GOVERNMENT

Dedicated to the memory of my mother,
Beatrice Ball

Performance Review in Local Government

ROB BALL

Ashgate

Aldershot • Brookfield USA • Singapore • Sydney

Published by
Ashgate Publishing Ltd
Gower House
Croft Road
Aldershot
Hants GU11 3HR
England

Ashgate Publishing Company
Old Post Road
Brookfield
Vermont 05036
USA

British Library Cataloguing in Publication Data
Ball, Rob
    Performance review in local government
    1. Local government - Great Britain - Evaluation
    I. Title
    351.4'1

Library of Congress Catalog Card Number: 98-71408

ISBN 1 84014 123 9

Printed in Great Britain by The Ipswich Book Company, Suffolk

Contents

Figures and tables

Acknowledgements

I am particularly grateful to Dr Claire Monaghan for making a major contribution to the research described in this volume. Without Claire's contribution, this book could never have been written. Thanks go to all my colleagues at the Department of Management and Organization at Stirling University for their support whilst working on this book. Also my thanks to the members and officers at Central Regional Council and Stirling Council whose discussions on policy matters greatly contributed to the background to this book. In particular, I should particularly like to acknowledge the support of Anne Wallace of Central Regional Council and Ann Strang of Stirling Council.

I would also like to thank those officers and members throughout the UK who generously contributed their time to the research work. The financial support of the Economic and Social Research Council is gratefully acknowledged. Thanks are also due to Elizabeth Fraser and Sharon Martin for typing the manuscript and converting it to camera ready form.

Finally I would like to thank my wife Moira and son Chris for putting up with my frequent unavailability whilst working on this manuscript.

Preface

As local government has become more policy driven and financially constrained, interest in performance review has increased. Such interest has recently been increased by the introduction of Best Value by the Government, since performance review is an integral part of this process.

This book attempts to place performance review in its appropriate political and managerial context. It also endeavours to establish its close relationship to the policy and service planning process. Existing work on performance indicators and the development of 'standard' performance review systems are considered before discussing the author's empirical work in the performance review area. This work fields a range of insights into the successful development and operation of performance review systems gathered from Authorities who are working in this area. Major problems and difficulties and potential further developments was also identified.

The impact of the Citizen's Charter on performance review in Local Government is also explored. The views of the author, that the way that the Charter has been applied to the local government area may prove damaging, are outlined.

In the final chapter likely future developments in the performance review field are examined. The principles of Best Value and the essential part played by performance review are highlighted. Owing to the introduction of Best Value, it appears that performance review work is likely to be an integral part of the work of all middle and senior managers in local government. It is hoped that this book will be of assistance in helping them tackle this task.

It is also hoped that undergraduate and postgraduate students studying public administration or public management will also find this book invaluable.

1 Performance review - the political and managerial environment

Introduction: the need for performance review

Organisations that operate in the traded sector of the economy have a range of measures available to evaluate their performance. Such measures include profit, market share and a range of financial ratios such as solvency and productivity ratios. Most of these performance measures are reasonably well established although their appropriate use still involves problems in interpretation and choice of a suitable timescale.

There are no such well established measures of performance in the non traded and public sector into which local authorities fall. Nevertheless, such approaches are necessary. If performance is not monitored then it is impossible to tell if reasonable progress is being achieved in delivering organisational objectives. Neither can the authority respond effectively to attacks from central government and elsewhere.

The need for performance review has long been recognised in local government. As far back as 1972 the Bains committee (which was advising on management structures following the 1974 local government reorganisation) advised setting up a specialist performance review sub-committee to complement the work of the policy and resources committee in achieving corporate objectives. In Scotland the Paterson committee (1973) suggested that performance review questions should be handled at the full policy and resources committee. Following local government reorganisation in the 1970s many authorities took the recommendation of the Bains and Paterson reports on board. Indeed, some commentators feel that in some cases authorities adopted some elements of these committee recommendations rather uncritically. In our studies we found a few systems that were introduced in the 1970s that were still in existence and that some current systems are modifications of 'earlier' systems dating from this time.

Performance review was also considered in the Layfield report on local government finance published in 1976. This report was focused mainly on issues relating to local government finance, but also touched on efficiency and 'value for money' questions. Performance review was considered by this committee to be a useful service to management, 'encouraging elected members to participate more effectively in the accountability process'.

This book is concerned with the current state of the art with respect to performance review in British local authorities. It is based on a three year Economic and Social Research Council study, and focuses on experience of British local authorities in the performance review field, views of officers and members together with ideas for good practice.

It would clearly be rather myopic to focus on performance review in isolation. A number of issues are so closely associated with the performance review process that they have to be included in any comprehensive survey of this topic. Amongst these is the question of local authorities becoming a policy driven organisation. Without such an orientation the power of performance review becomes questionable. After all, if organisations have no idea what they are trying to achieve, why go to the effort of trying to monitor it? Planning issues relating to the development and implementation of policy objectives over a period of time are also closely related to performance review questions. Indeed, our studies indicate that the majority of local authorities had managed, to some extent, to integrate the operation of their performance review system with their planning system. Thus, we shall be exploring in depth the work of local authorities with both strategic planning and service planning systems.

These planning issues will be discussed in the next chapter. Further clarification of terms related to performance review will be presented in Chapter 3.

Becoming a policy led council

There is little point in a council trying to assess its performance unless it has some idea what it is trying to achieve. Without some kind of policy perspective, performance review is liable to become a meaningless bureaucratic chore.

Although politics is a dominant factor in running most local authorities, the statutory framework on which local authorities are based and which reflects corporate decision making may not easily facilitate this. Thus, even if a council is politically controlled it may not be policy led. Clearly, if policies are not properly specified, then performance review procedures will be ineffective. This problem was recognised in the Widdicombe report (1986).

> In summary local government institutions are in many respects poorly attuned to the modern political environment. The weakness has always existed but has been masked out by the successful operations of convention in a period of growth and relative consensus. More recently the extent and pace of political change has exposed this weakness. The political process, instead of fitting into a regulated framework within the local government system is tending to operate outside and at odds with the

system. At best this is causing uncertainty and instability. At worst power is being abused ... the local government system does not formally recognise the existence of politics.
(Widdicombe report, 1986, p63)

Councils that are 'political' but fail to become policy led either because of their problems of explicitly introducing politics into local authority structures (as described above) or through lack of will of the political group may exhibit the following features:

1   An excessive operational focus. Since members are unable/unwilling to get to grips with policy issues, attention focuses on operational issues with members trying to second guess managers.
2   A proliferation of committees and sub committees spending unnecessarily large amounts of time discussing routine business.
3   Because of the focus on operational issues a bureaucratic culture tends to develop.
4   Since the council is not proactive in pursuing its own policy initiatives it will be reactive, simply responding to outside events. Without a clear policy perspective it will tend to respond clumsily.
5   Given the existence of a policy vacuum, it will be difficult to establish a corporate response to issues. As a result it is likely that departmentalisation will be rife with director 'baronies'.
6   Chairs of committees will tend to become departmental spokespersons in the political group rather than vice versa.
7   Lack of a policy perspective will make it impossible to develop appropriate strategic approaches. This will result in a 'finance driven' authority.
8   Disappointment with lack of political progress in implementing the manifesto and delivering other political commitments will result in poor relationships between the group and its political party. Often because of their inward looking culture such authorities have poor relationships with the public.

Most readers of this book will recognise some of the above elements in councils with which they are familiar. Indeed the author was a member of a council that had such a perspective for many years. The perspective of this group was cogently summarised by the Times Educational Supplement (Scotland) 1986:

Central Region's Labour group represents not so much the Labour party of yesterday, but the Labour party of the day before yesterday.

The group were demoralised by their failure to make headway on developing a political perspective and decided to hold a two day seminar at a hotel in the countryside 30 miles distant from the council offices. Although such a proposal brought the usual accusations of 'junketing' from the press and opposition groups it was agreed essential as such an event in council offices could not be expected to generate an adequate level of commitment, attention or attendance. A facilitator from a nearby university was appointed to structure and draw out the discussion.

During the two days there was close examination of what the authority had been doing and some extremely plain speaking. Many members were disenchanted, feeling that they were putting considerable time and effort into their council work and yet, at the end of the day, felt that there was little concrete evidence of solid achievement. One particularly salutary exercise was an examination of the roads and transportation committee's agenda. Of 57 agenda items only three appeared to have any policy implications.

At the end of the meeting most members came to the conclusion that there was no prospect of becoming a policy led council unless operations were radically altered to allow the time and opportunity for developing policy issues. Opportunities existed to make such radical changes since the council was approaching a new election after which all convenerships and vice convenerships would be reallocated. In addition, the chief executive had already resigned and there would be the opportunity of appointing another one who might embrace this new agenda.

In the event far reaching changes were agreed. Firstly the committee structure was radically revised in a way to reduce the number of committees and to try to emphasise policy questions. The former policy and resources committee had been ineffective. It had met on two occasions in each cycle. The first meeting was intended to discuss policy issues. Sometimes, the agenda for this meeting contained details of new legislation, but more often than not it was cancelled 'because of lack of business!'. The other committee meeting, called the 'Minutes' meeting, involved desperately picking over the bones of other committee's minutes to identify issues that could be deemed to have some policy significance. Thus the approach of this committee was reactive and nugatory and in order to try to develop a strong policy framework it was suggested that a separate policy committee should be instigated. Although now separated from resources, the committee would still nevertheless operate within the overall resource context of the council.

Otherwise committees and particularly sub committees were drastically pruned as can be seen from Figures 1.1 and 1.2 which show the council's committee structure before and after restructuring. A feature of this was that all resource committees (finance, lands and buildings and personnel) were absorbed into a new 'resources' committee.

Reduction of the number of committees is in itself only a partial solution if all the agenda items are simply redistributed amongst the new committees. There is an additional need for pruning the agendas themselves. This was done by changing standing orders to delegate to officers many decisions which were simply routine applications of existing policy (e.g. admission of children to special needs schools). Many routine information items were also removed from committee agendas. It was still necessary to maintain accountability and in order to do this a document called the bulletin was issued which contains a record of actions taken on the matters now delegated to managers. Members were entitled to question officers on such matters at council meetings. In the event few if any questions are ever in fact asked. Another important development was the introduction of pre-agenda meetings. This restored control of agendas to elected members.

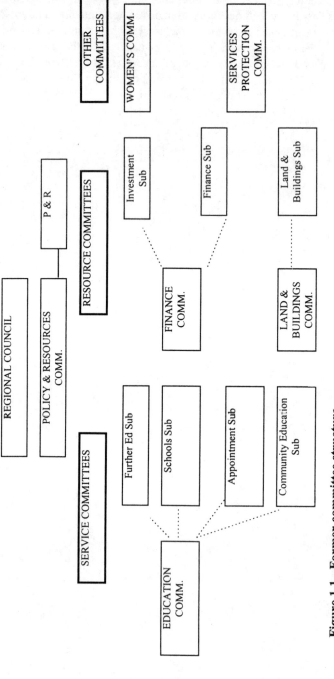

Figure 1.1 Former committee structure

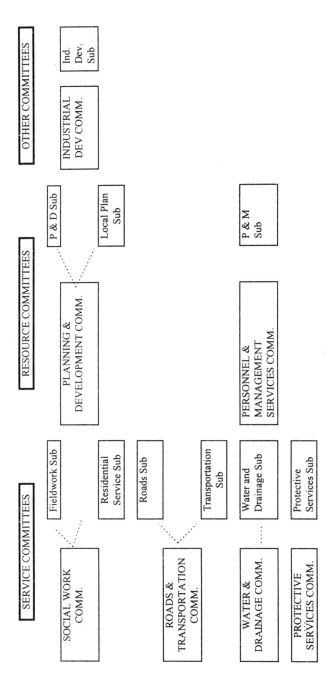

Figure 1.1 Cont'd

7

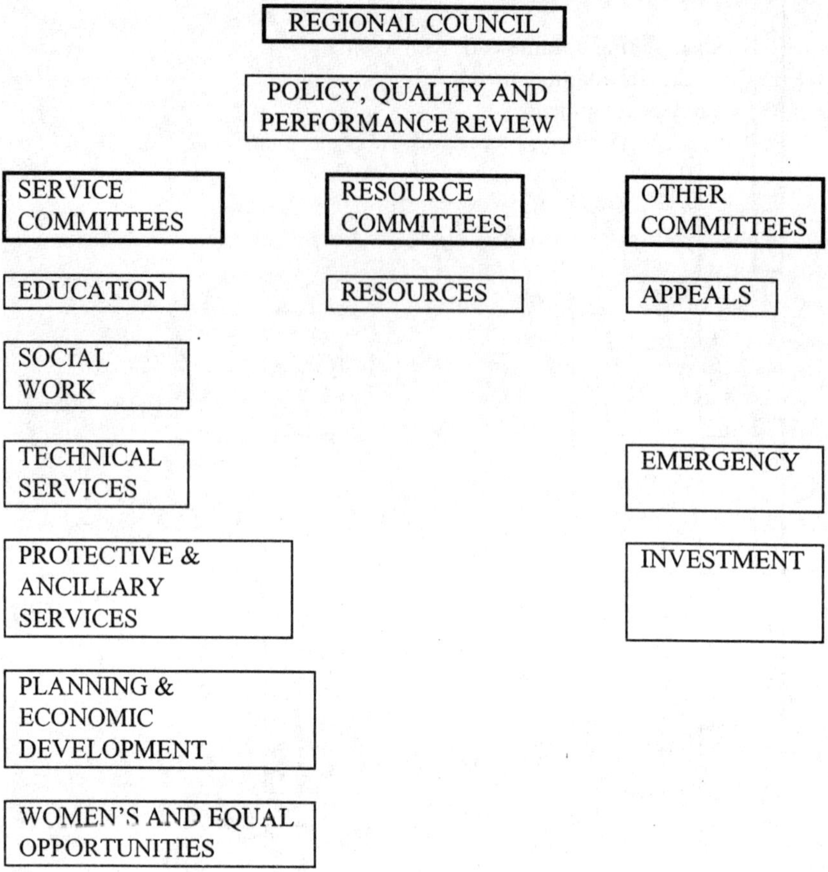

```
                    ┌─────────────────────┐
                    │  REGIONAL COUNCIL   │
                    └─────────────────────┘

                    ┌─────────────────────┐
                    │ POLICY, QUALITY AND │
                    │ PERFORMANCE REVIEW  │
                    └─────────────────────┘

┌─────────────┐        ┌─────────────┐        ┌─────────────┐
│ SERVICE     │        │ RESOURCE    │        │ OTHER       │
│ COMMITTEES  │        │ COMMITTEES  │        │ COMMITTEES  │
└─────────────┘        └─────────────┘        └─────────────┘

┌─────────────┐        ┌─────────────┐        ┌─────────────┐
│ EDUCATION   │        │ RESOURCES   │        │ APPEALS     │
└─────────────┘        └─────────────┘        └─────────────┘

┌─────────────┐
│ SOCIAL      │
│ WORK        │
└─────────────┘

┌─────────────┐                               ┌─────────────┐
│ TECHNICAL   │                               │ EMERGENCY   │
│ SERVICES    │                               └─────────────┘
└─────────────┘

┌─────────────┐                               ┌─────────────┐
│ PROTECTIVE &│                               │ INVESTMENT  │
│ ANCILLARY   │                               └─────────────┘
│ SERVICES    │
└─────────────┘

┌─────────────┐
│ PLANNING &  │
│ ECONOMIC    │
│ DEVELOPMENT │
└─────────────┘

┌─────────────────────┐
│ WOMEN'S AND EQUAL   │
│ OPPORTUNITIES       │
└─────────────────────┘
```

Figure 1.2   New committee structure

As we have seen, setting a framework within which policy development may take place is essential. In addition to this it is essential to set up mechanisms for generating policy developments.

One method employed very successfully was the member/officer group. This was used to develop policy in a number of areas such as transportation, under fives, Europe etc. Member/officers groups usually consisted of four officers and four members (all from the majority group). Membership of groups was based on an individual's potential contributions rather than status (often third or fourth level officers were involved). Convenors of the relevant committees were excluded. Officers involved had their normal workload reduced and sometimes received secondment from their normal duties. In practice, this structure worked well and very valuable policy documents were produced. In fact the transportation policy document 'All Change' received national recognition. It was also recognised that appropriate performance review systems would be an essential part of ensuring effective policy implementation.

In a number of other areas policy development was achieved by major internal review. Such reviews took place in development and planning, technical services and education.

In the next section we shall review the political and economic climate, in which performance review takes place.

Performance review: the political environment

Clearly, in considering this topic we have to take account of both the *national* and *local* political environment. We shall first consider the national political environment.

The national political environment

The former Conservative Government propagated the idea widely that the public sector is inherently less efficient than the private sector. Local government down the years was particularly singled out for vitriolic attacks and abuse from government ministers, of which the following is a typical example:

> By 1979 Local Government had become a barely controllable free wheeling employment machine which for year after year had been run largely for the benefit of the machine minders.
> (Heseltine, 1987, p43)

Crude prejudices of this kind, however, were given intellectual underpinning by the proponents of public choice theory. Public choice theorists apply economic type approaches in which participants adopt utility maximising behaviour to the political process. Stated crudely this means that politicians achieve their goals of attaining office by exclusively carrying out programmes which please most voters. Governments which wish to maximise political support will carry out those acts of spending which attract the most votes supported by those acts of financing which loses the fewest votes (Downs, 1957). The implication of the above is that political systems should converge and that politicians never seek office to carry out particular policies for ideological reasons; they simply offer policies which enable them to gain office for the rewards of income, prestige and power.

Although the basic tenets of this theory may seen bizarre (particularly to elected members in local government whose rewards in terms of income, prestige and power are rather meagre) and the empirical evidence supporting it is weak (Monaghan and Midwinter, 1993), this theory has been very influential in right wing circles. Indeed, the introduction of the community charge (poll tax) and the limitation of rebates to 80 per cent were justified by arguments related to public choice theory.

Other attacks on local government related very much to performance review type issues. Some of these centred on the lack of a bottom line or profit motive in local government. Although the following quotation is from the Audit Commission (1986), it nevertheless typifies the kind of thinking which was found in Government circles:

> Making a profit or at least avoiding a loss, is thus a convenient performance indicator which covers efficiency and effectiveness in one term ... In local government on the other hand there is generally no profit motive to act as an indication of performance.
> (Audit commission, 1989, p3)

The above indicates a fairly naive understanding of the private sector. A company working exclusively to profit as a measure of performance would be heading for serious trouble. For example, a company might be making substantial profits from a number of products reaching the end of their product life cycle but be in difficulty because it had no potential new products in the pipeline. Also, at least in the short term, profit levels can be strongly influenced by accounting assumptions or behaviour that may have serious longer term consequences such as cutting Research and Development. Thus, in practice, analysts have a whole battery of indicators to judge the performance of private sector companies. Also, sudden unexpected insolvencies (e.g. Polly Peck) indicate that even the most sophisticated analysis is not entirely foolproof. Olsen (1987) succinctly sums up the kind of simplistic thinking behind the Audit Commission statement:

The image of the private sector is seldom based on empirical observations of how that sector actually works Rather, it is taken from how introductory text books in business administration say it should work. (Olsen, 1987, p3)

Midwinter and Monaghan (op. cit., p101), suggest a more self-serving hidden agenda behind the continual strident reference to local government inefficiency. They believe that this allowed the government to call for expenditure cuts without accepting the political opprobrium for eroding services. The government could then claim that financial savings can be delivered without depleting service levels through efficiency improvements. It would be very difficult to counter this argument without appearing to defend waste and inefficiency.

Whatever the merits of the above argument there can be little dispute that local government was facing continued pressure to justify its performance from a hostile government. We believe that appropriate performance review systems can help to demonstrate accountability and appropriate progress towards the council's goals. This may provide some defence against the types of attack mentioned above. Indeed, Butt and Palmer (1985) believe that performance measurement in local government acts as a proxy for the profit criterion in the private sector.

The national context continued: the role of the audit and accounts commission

The 1982 Local Government Act established the Audit Commission for local authorities in England and Wales. Under this legislation the role of auditors of local authority accounts was extended to include a duty to be satisfied that:

The local authority has made proper arrangements for securing economy, efficiency and effectiveness.

A similar remit was extended to Scottish auditors by the Local Government Act 1988.

Thus, powers of auditors were extended well beyond that of the simple probity audit. These enhanced audits were outlined by the 1980 Green paper dealing with the role of the comptroller and auditor general.

Value for money audit A value for money audit is an examination of economy and efficiency to bring to light examples of wasteful, extravagant or unrewarding expenditure, failure to maximise receipts or financial arrangements detrimental to the exchequer and weaknesses leading to them.

Effectiveness audit An effectiveness audit is an examination to assess whether programmes or projects undertaken to meet established policy goals and objectives have met those aims.

Whilst there is a clear distinction between the value for money and effectiveness audits with the former focusing on waste avoidance and the latter with goal attainment, they are now colloquially synonymous.

Clearly, attempts at securing the 'proper arrangements' referred to above clearly may lead to the examination of performance review procedures.

Armed with their statutory powers the Audit Commission has been much more vocal than the Accounts Commission in calling for performance review procedures. They have published a number of technical manuals on performance review but have generally failed to link review with the political process. The Audit Commission (1988) defines the review process as comprising four main stages:

1   Determine performance measures.
2   To set targets for that performance and to monitor achievement against these.
3   To review selectively those areas where performance does not come up to expectation.
4   To take action arising from the review process.

Further detailed discussion of the type of performance review systems proposed by the Audit and Accounts Commission is given in Chapter 4.

In May 1997, after eighteen years in office, the Conservative Government was defeated.

The local political environment

The author's research has uncovered a wide range of performance review schemes initiated by local authorities. It would be wrong to imply or assume that the majority of these have been devised in response to central demands since most considerably exceed the rudiments of efficiency and effectiveness required to satisfy the Audit and Accounts committee. Our investigations further revealed that most schemes have been developed locally in response to specific needs.

We have identified a number of factors driving this interest.

Fiscal stress In its introduction to 'performance review in local government - a handbook for auditors and local authorities', the Audit Commission argued that:

> Performance review in local government has developed as a result of ... pressures on public spending at a time of changing social and economic circumstances.
> (Audit Commission, 1986, p3)

There may be some merit in this argument. Financial stringency necessitates difficult decisions and this forces attention to be focused on core objectives. A well devised performance review system can usefully facilitate the rationalisation process in such an instance. However, we would guard against any close association being developed between performance review and fiscal containment. Performance review is about maximising the use of resources and demonstrating progress towards goals and objectives. It should not be used primarily as a tool for delivering the latest round of cuts. Unfortunately it may on occasion be used in this way. In our studies the director of social work in a large English county council suggested that he suspected 'that performance review at his authority had an element of finessing cuts'.

Compulsory competitive tendering (CCT)

The process of putting specific service areas out for competitive tender demands that authorities clearly state the specification and required level of provision of services. Ensuring that this contract is fulfilled necessitates the monitoring of service delivery against targets and this has inevitably led to a more performance orientated atmosphere emerging. This is to an extent also the case with *service level* agreements where service departments and central department come to agreement about the level and nature of services that will be delivered and their likely cost.

Political decentralisation

Decentralisation can extend to the democratic process itself. Within the council this may involve devolving more powers to committees to take decisions within the authority's corporate framework. Political decentralisation can involve the public directly in local decision making. One form of this is the local area committee where members of the public, elected members and local area managers who hold the service budget for the local area, make decision about matters concerning their area.

Bradford Metropolitan Borough Council have a system of *area panels*. Five panels are based on parliamentary constituencies. Each has a membership of six councillors and will set priorities for its area within the council's overall policy and make recommendations to the relevant committees. Area panels are supported by area liaison groups representing interest groups and organisations which already exist in each area e.g. voluntary sector, business community and public service providers (e.g. police and health authority) and representation from the neighbourhood forum. Neighbourhood forums are planned to reflect individual and community interests and are designed to give individual communities a voice in the strategic and operational proposals for the area via the area panels and the council's formal committee structures.

It is obviously important that the scope for decision taking by such bodies will need to be clearly thought through so that they do not end up in a position where they are taking decisions contrary to corporate aims.

It is generally accepted that local government is more politicised than in the past. As recently as 1965 the Maud committee found that two-thirds of all councillors considered that council work would be done better without the party system. Twenty years later attitudes had dramatically changed; the Widdicombe committee carried out a survey which showed that 63 per cent of councillors agree rather than disagree that 'the first concern of the elected member is to implement the party manifesto' (87 per cent of Labour councillors and 61 per cent of Conservatives). The reasons for this shift are a matter for conjecture, but the greater degree of polarisation in society together with the continuous battle which central government has waged against local government may provide some explanation. Increased politicisation has initiated a change in councillors' attitudes. Many members are no longer content with limiting themselves to their civic roles or 'minding the shop' but now place much more emphasis on achieving what they regard as their most important political objectives. A well defined performance review system is one method of monitoring progress towards the achievement of political goals and thus has attractions for members. In fact in a number of councils the driving forces behind the implementation of review processes has come from councillors.

The managerial environment

We have, for convenience, grouped managerial issues into this part of the chapter. It must be recognised, however, that the managerial and political environment of the public sector institution are intimately related. This is clearly recognised by Stewart (1990):

> It is a dangerous mistake to believe that political processes and management processes are opposed to each other or can be separated. Effective management of an organisation has to be grounded in the purposes and conditions of that organisation and the political process sets the purposes and conditions of local government.
> (Stewart, 1990, p25)

If we accept the above, attempts to manage an authority as if it were not a political organisation is likely to lead to ineffective and inappropriate action. To quote Stewart again:

> Effective management cannot be based on a denial of the nature of the organisation to be managed.
> (p26)

Thus, it is necessary for local government to have management systems in which political and managerial processes are intertwined.

Although members' primary responsibility is for policy and officers for management, there is no way that it is possible to construct a rigid demarcation line between the two. Since a member is responsible for all the activities of the authority, he will wish to assure himself that effective management systems exist even though he/she should not normally get involved in detailed operational matters. Likewise, officers will normally be involved in the policy making process by offering advice, suggesting policy options, carrying out research, etc.

Currently, there are a number of significant changes taking place in the managerial environment within the public sector in general and local government in particular. We will outline these changes below and explore their likely implications for performance review systems.

1   Restructuring the organisation into one with fewer departments and fewer chief officers

There has been a growing trend for local authorities, and particularly the smaller district councils, to restructure themselves into fewer large departments with a consequential reduction in the number of chief officials. Maybe the most extreme example of this occurred at Rossendale District Council as reported in the local government training board's 'management innovation in the smaller shire districts'. In Rossendale in the 1980s, following a palace revolution within the ruling Conservative group, a new leader ruthlessly restructured the council into only two departments and chief officers. These comprised a borough director who had overall responsibility for the authority and particularly for financial, legal and administrative matters and a director of operating services responsible for all service operations. Senior managers in leisure, housing etc., were no longer chief officers, but were, instead, section heads.

In our visits to local authorities we did not find any restructuring proposals as radical as the above, but we did find many authorities who were undergoing major restructuring. For example in Wyre District Council the directorate had been reduced to four: the chief executive and three central directors. These were heads of central services, development services and community services. These four constituted a management board who worked on strategic problems and tried to handle problems of coordination.

Reading Borough Council had, over a number of years, gradually reduced their number of departments from seven to six and had plans for a further reduction to five. This is in line with the authority's corporate plan to produce a structure to fit the task and to structure around the task rather than around the profession. A 'lean and flat' structure is also envisaged.

15

Flatter management structures are to be found increasingly in both private and public sectors. Even the police have not been immune, with recent changes eliminating two levels in the hierarchy.

Flatter management structures result in fewer levels of management hierarchy through which decisions have to be passed up and down. Clearly this helps to facilitate a more devolved management structure. In a devolved management structure decisions are taken and operations are carried out at the lowest appropriate level in an organisation. An effective devolved management system should result in more responsive decisions, strengthened accountability and better use of resources. As a part of the move to a more devolved management structure, many authorities have drastically revised their chief officer structure of director, depute, assistant (sometimes even chief assistant) to a 'head of service' structure.

For example, Figure 1.3 indicates how Central Regional Council changed their management structure in the economic development and planning field reducing both numbers of posts and flattening the structure.

Management devolution has important consequences for training. Since lower levels of management would have more discretion over decision making, it is important that appropriate training is provided. Such training should cover both corporate issues, since the manager requires to understand the corporate context in which his decisions are to be made and training in particular skills.

Many authorities have responded by providing appropriate training facilities for these new responsibilities. Bradford Metropolitan Borough Council gives its managers a two day programme covering corporate issues entitled 'the challenge of community government'. This programme covers a wide range of corporate issues including a strategic overview of the organisation, the challenge of community government, the anti-poverty strategy and the area panel initiative (Bradford's decentralisation initiative).

At Newcastle the decentralised management initiative involves devolved budgeting, therefore junior managers are given comprehensive training on budget management. At Kent County Council hundreds of managers are given training in performance review systems.

Another facet of decentralisation is attempting to make services physically more accessible to the public. The delivery of some local government services has traditionally been delivered on a local basis, e.g. education and social work. Others, however, have often not been decentralised and it may be necessary for an elector to make a lengthy journey to headquarters to pursue that matter in which they are interested.

This type of physical decentralisation may be facilitated by providing a 'one stop' access point at which access and information about a wide range of services can be provided. If local government in the area is of the 'two tier' variety, then it is much better if the local access point covers services provided by both authorities. Again this has staff training implications, in that whoever is employed at the local access point will be required to receive training to gain knowledge of a wide range of council services.

Previous Structure

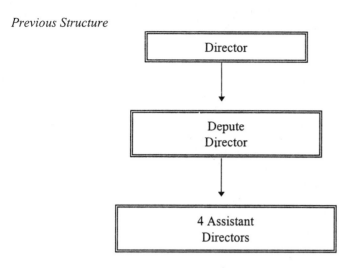

Revised Structure

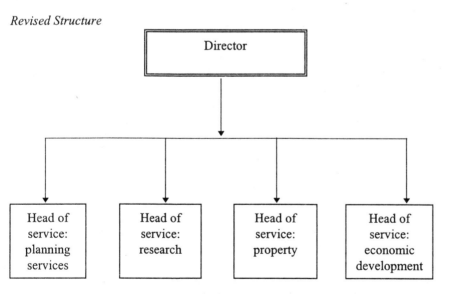

Figure 1.3   Previous and revised structure

A complaint that is often heard is that, in the past, local authority services reflected too closely the needs and interests of producers. To counteract this, many authorities have tried to become more user focused and to get more information in the form of surveys on the needs and views of service users.

Although local authorities may have been elected on a political programme, it should not be automatically assumed that the process gives complete information about citizens' views on services. Many voters vote on the basis of ideological commitment rather than current views on the quality of the authority's services. Elected members, through their surgeries, have useful information about users' views, but inevitably this can be sporadic and impressionistic. Therefore, many authorities have tried to gain more information about constituent views using either user panels or surveys.

Brent Borough Council is an example of an authority that carries out a range of survey work. This council has published a register of surveys (February 1991), which carries a brief description of all survey work carried out in recent years. One of the most important was a residents' attitude survey from the early 1990s which was conducted by MORI and included just over 1,000 adults aged 18+. The results of this report indicated high levels of dissatisfaction with services in the borough. The majority of respondents did not believe they were getting value for money, believed that the council was unhelpful and out of touch with the community. Action taken as a result of this survey included the development of 'Brent Council and the community: a programme of action 1990-94'.

A further survey covered an examination of parents' attitudes towards the choice of secondary school for their children. Parents were asked about the information they had received on the school of their choice and about the most important reasons for their choice. Some valuable information emerged from this survey. When asked to prioritise factors taken into account when choosing a school, proximity to home emerged as the most important factor, followed by good examination results and good discipline. Nearly one-third of residents were sending their children to schools outside the borough. Main reasons given were that they found out of borough schools had better academic standards, that they had been impressed by a particular school or that their child had brothers and sisters already at the school.

There is still some resistance to the notion of trying to obtain more information about users' views. The author was convenor of a committee which authorised a market research study costing £30,000 into user satisfaction with the council's services (the council's budget totalled £250 million). He was subsequently castigated in the local press for 'wasting public money'. There was a clear implication that the council should automatically 'know' what its constituents' views were. This provides an interesting contrast with the private sector where presumably one would be likely to suffer criticism for failing to undertake market research.

If one carries out survey work, it is very important to take action based on the outcome of the survey. Failure to do so will lead to disinterest and disillusion.

It is also very valuable to repeat surveys over a period. This helps to monitor if progress is being achieved with particular problem areas.

The Accounts Commission's paper 'narrowing the gap' (1988a) suggests that there are a whole series of formal steps to be taken in developing a user focus. These steps are outlined as follows:

1   Identifying what people's needs are and recognising that different groups have different needs.
2   Designing the service to meet needs.
3   Being clear about what is to be delivered.
4   Delivering the promised service.
5   Tackling performance.
6   Correcting failures quickly and efficiently.

A greater user focus also has implications for changing the prevailing corporate culture. There is also again an emergent training need. This is particularly important for front line staff who have the main contact with the public and who contribute greatly to the so-called 'transactional quality' of the service.

There is, however, an obvious danger in all this that local authorities will be looked upon from an excessively 'consumerist' standpoint. Local authorities are not simply bodies providing a range of miscellaneous services for individual 'consumers'. Indeed, consumers of some services such as the police would perhaps prefer not to be ones. It has to be recognised that many services such as police, planning, and transportation are provided collectively for the community as a whole, rather than for individual consumers. To evaluate such services in a consumerist way can lead to serious distortions. An example of the dangers of this approach is the tendency to evaluate performance of planning departments on the time taken to make decisions on planning applications, rather than the quality of the decision in relation to the interests of the community as a whole.

4   The enabling authority and the management of fragmentation

The original concept of the enabling authority was developed by John Stewart (see Clarke and Stewart, 1988).

Stewart's concept of the enabling authority is that of an authority that is concerned with all matters concerning its citizens and their welfare and would not merely confine itself to a service delivery role. In other words an enabling authority would consider itself to be much more than the sum of its services. Such an authority would be prepared to cooperate and network with other agencies in the private, public and voluntary sectors in meeting the needs of its citizens. Such a role did not necessarily imply any dilution in the authority's service delivery role, but that its scope would extend well beyond it. The authority would become, in the fullest sense 'a Local Government'.

The enabling concept has, however, been hijacked by the political right wing to such an extent that the word 'enabling' has become a code word for privatisation and opting out of services. In this version of the enabling authority, the authority delivers as little service as possible itself but buys in services from (usually) private sector suppliers and monitors their delivery. The most extreme version of the enabling authority was the apocryphal one of Nicholas Ridley, which met once per year to have lunch and decide which private sector suppliers should receive contracts for the next year (presumably this council never bothered to meet to monitor performance!).

The enabling idea, however, does have its limitations; for example an authority may draw up its housing plans. Implementing such a plan, however, may present great difficulties if the authority has no housing stock of its own and it is continually having to carry out its operations through third parties.

The enabling idea, however, is only one idea that has fragmented the management of local authorities. Compulsory competitive tendering has, in a number of service areas, separated the specification of service levels from delivery for a number of manual services. Proposals were afoot to extend this legislation to other areas of professional services. These proposals may have presented great difficulties because of problems of transferring the knowledge base. The introduction of quangos, either to take over or run in tandem with local authority services (for example Scottish Homes, or local enterprise companies) has also fragmented authorities' work as has the arbitrary taking over of areas of local Authority services (e.g. further education) by central government.

The overall effect of all this is to replace the multi-purpose authority with a network that involves specification of service and collaboration. These changed circumstances make it necessary to give greater emphasis to skills such as negotiation and persuasion.

According to Alexander (1991), however, the great difficulty with all these changes is that they detract from the notion of accountability and therefore threaten the future integrity of the local government system.

A further internal fragmenting development is the introduction of service level agreements when service departments negotiate specific levels of service and cost provided by central departments.

The above developments indicate that we have come a long way from the days when levels of local government service were reached by 'fudging'. Some would argue that we have now gone overboard and forced management in local government into a narrow, inflexible, legislative framework.

Implications of management change for performance review

Many of the above factors highlighted here underline the need for further development work in the performance review field.

The first is related to decentralisation. From a corporate perspective the danger of decentralisation is that, if not properly managed, it may lead to a loss of control (Perrow, 1977). Performance indicators provide a way of monitoring the operation of the devolved unit to ensure that it is continuing to operate according to guidelines and within corporate policies. As noted by Carter (1994), there can be a problem if the devolved unit does not own its own indicators.

The purchaser/provider split, CCT etc. has also established a need for appropriate performance review. The fact that a service is completely specified makes the monitoring of performance a much more straightforward task. The fact that services may be provided by external agencies makes proper monitoring more essential.

A final factor is the stronger user focus. Since we are no longer restricted to considering service delivery, the focus then shifts towards the outcome of the service. In this situation, performance review will be required to allow the service to be effectively monitored.

Summing up

In this Chapter we have outlined the need for performance review in UK local government and placed its development in its historical, political and managerial context. In the following chapters we shall consider the performance review process in more detail, and particularly focus on relationships with the strategic and service planning process.

2 Strategic and service planning

Background

As discussed in the previous chapter, performance review, if it is to be meaningful, needs to be related to the strategic and service aims of the council. If these have not been established, then it is dubious whether it is worthwhile embarking on establishing a performance review process. To quote from Drucker (1973):

> If you don't know where you are going then any plan will do.

Smith, Arnold and Bissell (1991) define the strategic planning process as:

> The process both of examining present and future environments, formulating organisational objectives and making, implementing and controlling decisions focused on achieving those objectives in present and future environments.
> (Smith, Arnold and Bissell, 1991, p3)

We should note the emphasis on the formulation and achievement of objectives and taking account of current and future environments in which the organisation is likely to operate.

Benefits of the strategic planning approach in the private sector are clear; the economic environment in which business operates is constantly changing. Moreover, the appearance of new markets and new technologies create unexpected opportunities and threats. An effective strategic plan should enable short term decisions to be taken that are consonant with the organisation's long term welfare. Furthermore, management decision making should be proactive, taking control of the organisation's destiny rather than continually reacting to external events and pressures (the so called 'fire brigade' approach). We shall now consider the strategic plan of the International Wool Secretariat (IWS).

The IWS exists to optimise the profitability of wool growers in Australia, New Zealand, South Africa and Uruguay. It was set up because it was believed that such countries could promote the demand for wool collectively better than individual countries acting on their own behalf.

In the five year strategic plan a number of external factors are taken into account. One of the most important is lack of growth in demand for fibres in general which indicates a greater need to gain market share. Other factors include technological changes resulting in improved quality performance and aesthetics of synthetic fibre, synthetic fibre-making's influence on premium markets, volatile exchange rates, changing lifestyles and emergence of developing countries as manufacturers and consumers of wool products.

A number of strategies are developed to try to achieve IWS objectives in the context of this environment. In addition, a number of critical key issues are highlighted together with appropriate action to be taken. These key issues are:

1   Market conditions threatening real price of wool, giving rise to need to control threats through increasing demand pressure for wool in carefully selected ways.
2   Some of its sponsors wishing to fund IWS in different ways.
3   Ensuring optimal research in R and D programmes in wool fibres and textile technologies.
4   Developing appropriate management information systems to monitor key elements of the strategic plan.
5   Building demand in developing countries.

The difference between strategic planning in the public and private sectors

It is possible to produce a general model of the strategic planning process that is likely to be valid for both the public and private sectors. (Figure 2.1).

Although the outline of the process may be valid for both public and private sectors, important differences do exist.

For example, in analysing the environment of the public sector organisation it may not be sensible to think about the competitive stance of the organisation except in a number of specialised situations. Public sector organisations do not have the option of opting out of a product or market merely because the environment appears unfavourable. In fact, market failure is more likely to cause the public sector to opt in. Again, strategic alternatives such as seeking out new markets or introducing new technologies may not exist in many parts of the public service. Furthermore, the process would normally be driven by a political imperative:

Strategic management in the public domain expresses values determined through the political process in response to a changing environment. It requires its own model.
(J. Stewart and S. Ranson, 1994, p55)

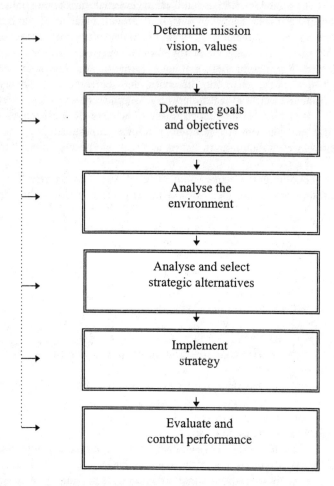

Figure 2.1   The strategic planning process

History of strategic planning in British local authorities

Before the late 1960s little or no strategic planning took place in British local authorities. Many authorities were simply loose collections of separate services ruled by director baronies. A county, town or borough clerk tenuously tried to hold such organisations together but attempts to coordinate activity and act corporately or to anticipate change were rare.

24

Both the Maud committee (1967) on the management of local government and the later Bains committee recommended coordination of the work of committees and officers. Structural changes were proposed to enable these recommendations to be implemented such as setting up a policy and resources committee, introduction of a chief executive and management team. Development of strategic planning was also proposed and the Paterson report on local authority management in Scottish authorities suggested a 'policy plan' as the master from which all other plans of the local authority should be derived.

Many authorities did introduce such strategic plans following local government reorganisation in the late 1970s. By the end of the decade, however, there was widespread disenchantment with this approach. A number of reasons have been suggested for this. Caulfield and Shultz (1989) suggested that many systems were over elaborate and were based on a weighty and cumbersome system called programme planning and budgeting system (PPBS); the purpose of which is to relate all budget expenditure to outputs. Such systems tended to fall apart under the weight of data required to operate them. Other reasons that have been suggested for the apparent lack of success of strategic planning during this period include:

1   Allegations of 'paralysis by analysis'.
2   Failure to think through the politics of planning.
3   Economic disruption during the 1970s caused by other crises and high inflation producing a generally turbulent environment with consequential crisis management.
4   Growth of conviction politics and obsession with short-term 'economy', narrow 'efficiency' and 'enterprise' (enforced competition).

Whatever the real reason, at the end of this period strategic planning was generally regarded as yet another management panacea such as management by objectives that had been tested and failed.

In spite of such negative experiences, however, interest in strategic planning revived during the 1980s. The Audit Commission has been a consistent champion of strategic planning. The first volume of its handbook 'Improving economy, efficiency and effectiveness in local government in England and Wales' published in 1983 highlighted strategy as one of the seven basic elements necessary to secure good overall management of a local authority. The 1989 handbook states that:

> An authority should be able to relate long term changes in service delivery to financial and staffing resources over a medium term three year timescale. To do this a planning process of more than one year and a performance review system are needed in addition to the one year budget and all three systems should be inter related.
> (Audit Commission, 1989)

Thus interest in strategic planning revived and some of the lessons of earlier approaches were taken on board. As in the private sector, strategic plans now tended to be much more focused and less all embracing. Some authorities adopted an approach of identifying a number of key issues. As Stewart (1991) has commented:

> If strategic planning is everything, it is nothing.
> (Stewart, 1991, p6)

Strategic planning: policy development and the manifesto

In the first chapter we discussed the importance of an authority developing an appropriate policy orientation. As we saw from the quotation from Stewart and Ranson, strategic management in the public domain expresses values determined through the political process. It is important therefore that a strategic plan should do this. A political party's manifesto gives broad objectives and policy initiatives that the party, should it become an administration, would wish to pursue. A manifesto is not, however, a strategic plan; it usually does not have timescales for delivery of commitments or explicit sets of priorities. If the strategic plan is to reflect political priorities it must properly take the manifesto into account.

It may be useful to carry out an analysis of the manifesto. This has to be done with some caution; it has to be constantly borne in mind that a good manifesto is more than simply a rag bag of isolated commitments. Whilst continuously bearing this in mind, however, the following analysis is perhaps helpful in facilitating a discussion around priorities. This approach divides statements in the manifesto into four kinds: new commitments, consolidation, declaratory statements and procedural measures. We shall now define the above using as examples statements from the manifesto of one of the parties standing in the 1994 election for Central Regional Council.

These are outlined below.

New commitments

These are commitments which commit the council to introducing a new development or activity. The following is an example from this manifesto:

> A quality assurance system will be introduced which will be aimed at supporting schools in carrying out self evaluation and self improvement and in building on the progress that is currently being made. The system will also provide genuine information on the quality of education in our schools.

26

Not all new commitments require additional resources, although almost certainly some will do so. The need to acquire sufficient resources is one of the reasons that new commitments will need to be phased in over a period of time. Thus, likely resource implications should be noted at this time.

Consolidation

These are activities which have already been introduced but with which there is a perceived need for further development. An example of this is:

> We will continue to develop safety schemes to protect pupils from the danger of traffic in and around schools.

Consolidation may sometimes require additional resources.

Declaratory

This kind of statement is usually an expression of political commitment or values. For example:

> We remain committed to the principle of comprehensive education based on the view that every child and adult is of equal value and should have the opportunity to achieve their potential in a system based on partnership and cooperation.

Procedural

These statements related to issues that may be resolved by changes in procedures or developing new procedures. For example (teacher workloads):

> However, conscious of the excessive workloads for staff, we are committed to resolving the problem through the efforts of the joint working group which was established to investigate this issue.

We can analyse a section of the manifesto - 'working towards equal' opportunities in this way (Exhibit 2.1).

Exhibit 2.1
Working towards equal opportunities

We recognise that equality of opportunity is not an accomplished fact either in the Council's service delivery or its recruitment or promotion procedures. The 'glass ceiling' continues to block the promotion prospects of many women, while people with disabilities and members of minority ethnic communities need specialised services in transportation, access, information and advice.

In 1990 the Council set up a Womens' & Equal Opportunities Committee, serviced by a dedicated unit, bringing together issues of disability, gender, race and sexual orientation. 1994 marks a decade of Scottish Local Government Women's Committees and after 10 years there is little optimism for women in the culture of the market place. More than ever womens' & equal opportunities committees need to be protected against the threat of a hostile environment.

Commitment	*Type*
We will continue to support issues of equality by maintaining and developing the role of the present committee and unit. The development fund will be maintained and enhanced by mainstream budgets where possible.	*Consol*
Increased accessibility to buildings, transport, information and other services will be promoted.	*Proced*
The safety of women in the community will be of the highest priority and public awareness campaigns and multi-agency approaches to domestic violence will be supported throughout the services of the Council.	*Dec*
As the largest employer in the Region the Council will strive to increase the number of women in senior and middle management positions by extending employment monitoring to all services of the Council and developing equality awareness for officers and members.	*New*
A programme of 'Family Friendly' policies will be developed including childcare initiatives, flexible working patterns and review and extension of paternity and carers leave.	*New*

Continued support will be given to the multi-agency strategy in monitoring and combating racial attacks and harassment.	*Consol*
We will ensure that the implications of local government re-organisation for women, minority ethnic communities, disabled people and lesbians and gay men are brought into the centre of discussions.	*Proced*
We will support the continuation of COSLA's Equal Opportunities Committee and raise issues of national concern through it e.g. the treatment of rape victims in court, the rise of racism in Europe and the need for antidiscriminatory disability legislation.	*Consol/New*

Helping people with special needs

We believe in the right of all children and young people to receive a full and rounded education in an environment conducive to releasing their full potential. Particular are must always be taken to ensure that the requirements of those with special needs and their families are taken account of.

Commitment	*Type*
The Review of Special Educational Needs provision will be completed and revised through the consultation process. An implementation programme will be carried out with the involvement of parents and staff throughout.	*Consol*
We will expand extended learning support facilities to cover all secondary schools within the Region and develop provision to primary schools where resources permit.	*New/Consol*

The complete analysis of the manifesto yielded 25 new commitments, 36 consolidating commitments, 18 procedurals and 23 declaratory ones. It can be a useful exercise to set up small groups of members and (possibly) officers to draw up a list of priorities of the various new commitments. Discussions centring around the consistency (or lack of it) between the deliberations of different groups can make a useful contribution to gaining a 'feel' for priorities.

It must be emphasised again that a manifesto should not be regarded as simply a loose collection of miscellaneous commitments, the feel for priorities obtained by the above process must again be related to a corporate perspective. It is helpful in this respect if the manifesto itself is written from such a perspective. This was the case with the manifesto discussed earlier entitled 'in defence of local democracy' which had the following thematic subsections:

1   A sense of community.
2   Responsiveness and accountability to local communities.
3   Helping people and communities reach their full potential.
4   Creating and protecting jobs.
5   Protecting and working with local communities.
6   Working to improve and protect the environment.
7   Working towards equal opportunities.

Moreover, strategic planning should enable the council to handle better those corporate issues that cross the boundaries of more than one service department. Such strategies might include anti poverty strategy, environmental charters, under fives, community safety etc.

Stages of the strategic planning process

We shall now consider the strategic planning process as outlined in Figure 2.1 in some detail, working through each of the stages in turn except the final one which will be pursued in subsequent chapters.

Stage 1 determine mission, vision and values

As we shall see later, mission, vision and values have different definitions. We found that few authorities had declared all these and in many cases a degree of ambiguity existed between them (for example, what might be considered by one authority to be a mission statement might be regarded as a set of values by another one. This could lead to an intense philosophical debate which, perhaps, would not much clarify matters. What is important is that these are attempts by authorities to give a general statement concerning what they believe to be their reasons for existence, their core philosophy and the 'business' they are in. These points should be borne in mind in the following discussion.

Values These can be defined as those ideas that a group considers important and desirable. Values strongly influence corporate culture and influence the consistency of decision making.
    Epsom and Ewell Borough Council defines its values as:

1   Open accessible local government.
2   Importance of local identity.
3   Excellence in quality of service.
4   Importance of cost-effective use of resources.

5	Commitment to enhance the environment.
6	Commitment to reduce crime.
7	Economic prosperity.
8	Importance of caring for vulnerable sections of the community.

It could be argued that the above are perhaps too detailed and specific and therefore could perhaps better be regarded as objectives.

Central Regional Council were another authority who had attempted to express their core values and supporting principles. These were:

Core values	**Supporting principles**
Closeness to public	Easy access to services. Valuing and being responsive to: (i) the public; (ii) internal customers.
Delegated decision-making	Quick decisions on service delivery. Getting the best from employees within a framework of trust and accountability. Valuing and respecting individual employees.
Effective communication	An effective dialogue between the council and: (i) its public; (ii) its employees. Consulting and listening to public and employees.

Vision Vision is closely related to values, defining a clear vision involves asking what businesses we are involved in and providing a view of future progress.

Epsom and Ewell's vision statement is:

> Epsom and Ewell believe that the local community is best served by local decisions being made locally. It will continuously improve the service it provides by responding to those it represents in order to enhance the quality of life in the borough and secure a thriving community.

One of the clearest vision statements is that of Bradford Metropolitan Borough Council. To understand the context, it should be remembered that this vision was formulated following the defeat of an extreme right wing administration under the leadership of Councillor Pickles. This statement is:

31

The Council will transform itself from the Tory concept of Bradford plc which saw individuals as consumers and staff and services as commodities into a council which regards each individual as an integral and valued part of the wider community with a distinct identity. Problems will be solved through the partnership of those communities with their effective, efficient and caring council.

Mission An organisation's mission statement describes the purposes that distinguish it from other similar organisations. A mission statement should:

1   Define what the organisation is and what it aspires to be.
2   Distinguish it from others.
3   Serve as a framework for evaluating both current and prospective activities.

We have already seen the values and vision of Epsom and Ewell Borough Council. The mission statement is:

Epsom and Ewell Borough Council will continuously improve its services by listening and responding to the community it represents in order to enhance the quality of life in the borough.

Bradford Metropolitan Borough Council have a very clear mission statement which links back to their vision described earlier in this chapter:

The City of Bradford Metropolitan Council will develop its strategic empowering role through partnership with other external organisations. It aims to have the highest calibre staff and best managed organisation to enable:

1   the provision of quality services for the whole community through partnership and consultation.
2   The development of pride in Bradford's heritage past and its multi racial community.
3   The provision of services that reflect the differing needs of the multi racial community and the diversity of different areas within the district.

As we mentioned earlier, sometimes the definitions of value, vision and mission overlap; this is perhaps of secondary importance. The important point is that an authority makes some attempt to define and debate what its basic purposes really are.

Stage 2 goals and objectives

There is a need to relate the mission statement to the goals and objectives of an organisation. In principle, objectives are supposed to be rather more short range and tightly focused than goals, but in practice we found that many local authorities use these terms interchangeably. We again shall take two appropriate examples. Bath Borough Council from 'Bath at the Threshold of the 90s' set out the following goals:

Economic viability Maintain the economic fabric of the city and promote diversity in Bath's economy by encouraging established industries to remain, attracting new non land intensive ones and promoting Bath's special strengths.

Quality of environment Preserve and enhance Bath's unique environment by investing in conservation and statutory protection and education and lobbying. To minimise pollution, litter and physical deterioration and encourage community pride.

Excellence in housing provision Promote excellence in housing standards and provision for the people of Bath by: managing and maintaining the council's own housing to high standards; increasing provision of affordable and social housing for rent and ownership in cooperation with the independent and private sectors and positively encouraging the renovation of sub standard private housing.

Cultural and recreational activities Extend and improve cultural and recreational activities for all sections of the community and promote participation by residents and visitors.

Respond To the needs of the public (residents and visitors) more effectively, especially disadvantaged, disabled and isolated groups. Identify resources available within the community and develop them.

As a further example we may note Wyre Borough Council who talk in terms of objectives. The council's overall objective is to enhance the quality of life for residents and visitors to the borough by:

1   Promoting and enhancing the health, well-being and rights of individuals.
2   Promoting the social aspirations and encouraging a sense of community amongst residents of the borough.
3   Contributing to safe and pleasant environment.
4   Generating prosperity.

This will be done through the provision of efficient and caring services and through the close liaison and coordination of the various committees of the council.

Objectives may be further broken down and this may introduce the need for *prioritising* between objectives. The use of priority search techniques may enable this to be carried out.

We have seen earlier in this chapter how the election manifesto commitments were broken down into new, consolidating, declaratory and procedural commitments. It is clearly necessary to develop clear ideas of the relative priority of commitments which require additional resources. This will be the case with most new and some consolidating commitments.

Priority search techniques operate as follows:

1   All objectives appear in pairs with a line of around 50 circles between them.
2   Each objective appears three times, each time paired with a different objective.
3   For each pair the respondent shows his preference between two objectives by putting a mark in the line of circles. The nearer the cross is to one or the other end, the greater the relative degree of preference. A mark in the middle indicates relative indifference. For example, three of the pairs of statements are given below.

Extend family friendly policies and child care	OO⊗ OOO .... OOOOOO	Develop alternative care foster care befriending
Provide training to meet needs of all employees	OOOOOO ...⊗.... OOOOOO	Increased investment in traffic calming
Implement the special education needs review	OOOOOO .... OOOO⊗O	Invest in strategic sites for economic development

In the first pair, extending family friendly policies is much preferred to developing alternative care. In the second case respondents are indifferent between providing training to meet the needs of all employees and increasing investment in traffic calming. In the third, investment in strategic sites is preferred to implementing the special education needs review.

Statistical means are then used to rank the preferences of a group of respondents. The results of the survey should be independent of the particular pairing used providing each objective appears three times and is linked to a different objective on each occasion.

In the Central Region case, members of the majority group took part in the priority search exercise, ranking the new commitments identified by analysing the manifesto. The top six of the 25 new commitments were as follows (Table 2.1):

Table 2.1
Ranking of new commitments

Rank	Objective	Score
1	Increase investment in street lighting and footpaths	11.3
2	Develop road safety schemes for schools	12.3
3	Increased investment in traffic calming	14.3
4	Implement proposals from council's youth strategy	15.2
5	Implement special education needs review	15.2
6	Nursery education in place for all children in pre school year	15.6

This exercise gave some insight into where the available resources should be focused in the short term.

Priority search techniques have also been employed at Bradford, this time applied to the question of managerial devolution. Managers were asked to state from their experience what would need to happen for devolved management to become a practical reality in Bradford. Responses were turned into a series of 'statements' or 'solutions'. These were arranged against each other in pairs in the way that we have seen earlier and a set of priorities developed. Table 2.2 gives a list of priorities developed.

Table 2.2
Bradford priority search technique. Preferences of the 17 members of this subgroup

Item	Rank
Commitment of senior management to devolved management	1
Commitment of staff within SDUs	2
Authority equal to responsibility	3
Training of staff in SDUs	4.5
Closer dialogue with the customer	4.5
Clear identification of support service costs	6.5
Action from senior management	6.5
Clarity on devolved management throughout authority	8
Clear political statement	9
Increase trust by more open discussion	10
Having business plans accepted	11
Awareness of customer's needs/demands	12
Being asked what support services we require	13
Budget based on actual cost not pro-rata	14
Need to know what support services are available	15
SDU managers input into budget allocation	16
Ethics of internal recharging	17
Control over recharges	18
Respect for workforce below officer grade	19
Having a budget	20
Guaranteed budget for a year	21
Ability to go outside for support services	22.5
Need bargaining power	22.5
Exploration of income generation	24
Identification of recharges	25
Need to know who is the customer	26
Views of non SDUs on devolved management	27
More radical change	28
SDU input into client specification for CCT	29
Less radical change	30

SDU - Service Delivery Unit

Stage 3 analysing the environment

Private sector organisations, in drawing up their strategic plan, need to give due priority to the fact that they operate in an uncertain environment. Implications for changes in technology, products and the economy must be taken on board if a plan is to be realistic.

Although the external environment is different in the local government context, the environment is, nevertheless, also changeable. Factors contributing to this changeable environment include government and EC legislation, further CCT, changes in expectation and social behaviour and even technological change. Failure to take potential environmental changes on board will result in the authority simply reacting to these pressures rather than taking advantage of any opportunity that they might present or taking precautionary action to deal with potential threats.

It is important to try to carry out the analysis of the environment (sometimes called environmental scanning) in a coherent and consistent manner. A technique called PEST analysis (Smith, 1994, p53) is useful for providing such support.

PEST stands for Political, Economic, Social and Technical environment and this forms the structure for the environmental analysis.

Political This covers UK and EC legislation, together with priorities of the Government as outlined in its election manifesto.

Economic May involve looking at employment trends and forecasts, the financial situation of the council, together with levels of poverty and deprivation in the area.

Social Should include lifestyles of people in the area; mobility; demographics; expectation and attitudes. Residents' consumer surveys should give valuable information in this context.

Technical To what extent may technical changes influence future developments, e.g. developments in IT may facilitate further progress in devolved management.

Kent County Council is an example of an authority who has developed an environmental scanning process.

Case study for Stage 3: environmental scanning in Kent County Council

In 1989, when drawing up the medium term plan for 1991-92 to 1993-94, Kent County Council commissioned a study of the environment which would inform corporate policies over the planning period in question. The report provided analysis of future developments in the following areas:

Economic change

It was predicted that the UK economy would grow more slowly over the 1990s but that Kent's economy would perform much better than other parts of the country. Decline in housing construction and job losses in manufacturing would increase unemployment from its then very low levels.

Population change

It was noted that the pace of population change which accelerated during the mid 1980s was almost entirely related to migration effects (more people moving into Kent than moving out). Given the belief that such increases were related to the economic cycle and housing market conditions, some future retrenchment might be expected.

The following structural changes were predicted:

1   An increase in 0-4 year olds through to the mid 1990s and growth in 5-9 year olds throughout the 1990s.
2   A marked decline in the 15-19 year olds throughout the 1990s which will have impacts on the labour market, together with the further/higher education sector. A slower rate of decline was predicted after 1991, with modest growth continuing beyond 1996.
3   An overall increase in the section of the population of working age during the 1990s, notwithstanding the decline in younger age groups entering the labour force for the first time.
4   Significant increases in the elderly retired population (75+) are predicted during the 1990s, with implications for community care.

Transport

It was predicted that traffic growth in Kent would continue to outstrip national growth rates with consequential implications for both road capacity and highway maintenance. Traffic growth was being driven by Kent's favourable economic development prospects, together with its geographic position as a bridge to Europe. It was recommended that the consequential need for provision of additional infrastructure and other traffic management measures need to be balanced against research results showing the public becoming increasingly concerned about both environmental quality and the impact of congestion on the quality of life.

Legislative changes

Current and proposed legislation had potentially important implications for strategy. The implications of a whole range of legislation: Education Reform Act (ERA), Children's Act, Firearms (Amendment) Act, Police and Criminal Evidence Act, Local Government Act (competition) was both significant and long lasting. Just to take one example, the national curriculum was to be introduced over a seven year period.

Proposed changes to the Health Service, Community Care and the forthcoming Environmental Protection Act were all likely to have further serious implications for the authority.

Public expectation

The report points to growing public awareness of issues related to child abuse and education. There is a trend for service users to become more demanding with increasing concern for quality, the environment and leisure. Demands for service improvements, however, need to be balanced against the perceived wish of the electorate to contain local government expenditure.

European integration

It was suggested that the implications of the opening of the channel tunnel and the introduction of the single market should be taken on board. The implications of the latter may be particularly significant for trading standards.

It can be seen that the environmental scanning process outlined above provides essential underpinning for the strategic planning process. For example, predicted economic changes will have implications for planning and economic development. Population changes impact on provision in education and social work, while potential transport growth has implications for the environment, public transport and highways.

Internal environment assessment

The purpose of an internal environment assessment is to help discover those internal strengths and weaknesses which may include organisational factors, management style and methods, employee and personnel factors etc.

Stage 4 analyse and select strategic alternatives

A SWOT analysis (Smith, 1994, p97) can be helpful in helping to develop alternatives. This type of analysis is widely accepted in both public and private sectors. It can be used at both the corporate levels of an organisation and in generating service plans.

SWOT stands for:

Strengths Which may be resources, skills or other distinct advantages of the organisation (e.g. well located Council Offices).

Weaknesses Limitations or deficiencies in the resources, skills and capabilities of the organisation.

Opportunities Major favourable situations which enable the organisation to achieve its goals and objectives.

Threats Major unfavourable situation in organisation or service environment which will hinder achievement of objectives.

A SWOT analysis has a number of benefits:

1   It can contribute towards a systems analysis of the organisation and its environment.
2   It allows you to take stock of the organisational position and future requirements.

Bryson (1988) describes a SWOT analysis carried out on a major US city. Amongst the *strengths* he lists:

1   Political leadership of mayor.
2   Management professionalism, stability and freedom of action.
3   Orientation towards action and innovation.

Amongst the *weaknesses* he lists:

1   Organisation - too strongly organised along vertical lines without enough lateral overlays and external contracts.
2   City Council - not an effective policy making body.
3   Mayor - a leader not an effective manager.

Amongst *opportunities* he includes:

1   Access and transportation.
2   Economic development.
3   Organisation and service redesign as a result of funding shortages and other pressures.

Amongst *threats* he includes:

1   Revenue loss.
2   Poor national and regional economy.
3   Competition from other governments, regions and the private sector.

Stage 5 generating strategic alternatives

Execution of the SWOT analysis allows each authority to focus on its key issues and generating strategic alternatives.

We shall see later on the way that key issues have been developed for two local authorities.

Strategy selection involves quite different options from the private sector. We have already seen that an authority cannot in many situations opt out of providing a particular service since it may well have a statutory obligation to provide it. Nor can it simply take over or conduct a merger with another authority, although joint ventures are, in principle, possible. There are a number of possible processes that can be used for generating strategic alternatives. These include:

1   An officer process.
2   A member process.
3   A committee process.
4   Member/officer group.

An *officer process* may be quite successful in generating strategic alternatives, some of which may well be adopted as policy by the local authority. There may be a problem, however, in that a policy may not equate with members' political agenda or that not being involved in the process they fail to 'own' the policy. In these circumstances there is a danger that a policy, once adopted, may simply lie in a filing cabinet gathering dust, or that it is abandoned at the first hint of problems.

A *member process* may be fine, but without officer support may be lacking in technical judgement and expertise.

Anyone who has had experience of local government will realise that a committee process is useless for policy development. It can, however, play a useful role in monitoring the successful implementation of policy.

The member/officer group may, however, present a useful way forward. The author has been involved in some highly successful member officer group. The organisation of these groups had the following features:

1   The groups usually consisted of four members and four officers. Officers were chosen on the basis of their expertise and potential contribution to the group. Back bench members were usually included in the member team.

2   The groups were given very clear terms of reference and a definite time scale by which they had to deliver their report.

3   Real resources were invested into group activities. These were used for carrying out some studies externally (particularly where appropriate expertise was unavailable in-house) and for the secondment of officers.

4   Although both members and officers realised that they had their own specific responsibilities, the members of the group regarded themselves as a team rather than representing officer or member positions.

5   Attendance by the group at a conference early on, on a relevant topic area, is useful for bonding of the group.

6   It is useful to carry out studies internally, although consultants will often, if necessary, provide skills not available internally.

7   There was debate over whether opposition members should be invited to participate in the group. This was rejected for two reasons:

(i)   It is not the job of the opposition to help implement the strategies of the majority group. Taking part in a policy group would conflict with their major role of providing a critique of proposals when they are brought back to committee.

(ii)   The presence of opposition party members would inhibit frank discussion and consideration of innovative ideas. Instead, there is a danger that the group sessions might be more like council meetings with members defending entrenched positions.

8   Convenors of service committees were not included in the member/officer group. This was done since it was felt there was a danger that such an individual might inhibit development of alternatives by acting as a departmental representative. There is a downside to this, however. At some stage the strategic alternative selected is likely to have to be implemented by a service committee and if not 'owned' by the convenor, this can lead to problems.

Strategic plans in practice

At this point it will be useful to consider examples of two local authority strategic plans.

Kent County Council corporate plan

Kent's corporate plan is a relatively slim document of around ten pages or so. Although no clear statement of mission is given in this document, its stated function is to enable the authority to manage change in a balanced way in providing a clear policy direction and resource framework. Each committee of the council also has a medium term strategic plan.

We have discussed earlier in this chapter the council's approach to analysing the external environment. Studies are carried out in the area of economic change, population change, transport, legislative change, public expectation and European integration.

A paramount objective appears to be the perceived need to strike a balance between meeting needs caused by change and the council tax paper. A number of corporate priorities/key issues are outlined.

1 *Schools* Increase in the school building maintenance and improving the quality of teaching.

2 *Disadvantaged Groups* Top priority was to be given to those groups with the greatest need. Substantial new investment to cater for children with special needs was planned together with increased emphasis on child protection and accommodating the growing numbers of handicapped and mentally ill people requiring care.

3 *Physical Environment* Increases in the waste disposal budget are proposed to allow for rising costs and falling income. A doubling of the capital budget for highways was predicted.

4 *Emergency Services (fire and police)* It is planned to increase investment to ensure that these services are fully prepared for the opening of the channel tunnel

The plan also provides an overarching resource framework within which decisions may be taken.

Central Regional Council

Central Region's values have already been presented earlier in this chapter. The strategic plan also contains a set of goals. These were:

1 Promoting the economic well-being of its communities through employment creation and retention.
2 Helping individuals, families and groups and organisations to achieve their full potential.
3 Improving and promoting safety within its communities.
4 Delivering efficient, effective services of a high standard which are user friendly and accessible to its communities.
5 Ensuring equal opportunities for those individual groups or communities who are disadvantaged or who have special needs.
6 Involving our communities and representing their views in the process of reaching decisions, promoting local democracy and citizenship.

An extensive study of the environment is carried out. This includes *looking at the age distribution* of the population in which the number of children of school age is expected to remain static but numbers of elderly (75+ and 85+) are expected to rise, with consequences in a number of service areas. These are:

Family/household/personal characteristics Suggest more smaller households, more elderly and very elderly living alone, lone parents increasing (1 in 8 of all children in lone parent families, and 25% of all births to non-married parents).

Social conditions Reveal considerably increased differential in income in recent years, with a much larger proportion of the population living in poverty. It is calculated that one in four children live on or below the income support level as do a similar proportion of the elderly. Although housing conditions continue to improve, there is a relentless increase in homelessness. Strong relationships between adverse social conditions and poor health have also been established.

Work circumstances Continuing high levels of unemployment are noted (average of 11 per cent, 20 per cent for males in one of the districts making up the region). There is also an increasing proportion of part time workers, whose conditions continue to be greatly inferior to those of full time ones.

Transport Growth of car ownership was noted: 63 per cent of households having a car in 1991, compared with 57 per cent in 1981. Nevertheless, 60 per cent of households with pensioners and 72 per cent of single parents have no car. A further decline in the use of public transport is reported.

Environment Reductions in sulphur dioxide and lead emissions were noted, but acid rainfall in the west of the region is amongst the highest in the country. Increasing use of chemicals in agriculture and forestry was threatening to affect water quality. The need to move towards sustainability was highlighted.

Crime Although there had been a 60 per cent increase in crime between 1981 and 1991, it was still running 22 per cent lower than the national rate. Nevertheless, various surveys had shown that fear of crime had affected many people's behaviour and ability to enjoy where they live.

Changes in the legislative environment are also taken on board. Amongst these the most traumatic of these was the potential for local government reform. The future of the water and drainage services in the light of government proposals, delivering the service through publicly controlled boards was also a matter for concern. In addition, there was the proposed extension of CCT to 'white collar' posts, devolved school management, community care, European legislation and the potential effect of the Single European Market and economic and monetary union.

There were also internal factors that should be taken into account. These were the commitments to decentralisation, training and employee development and value for money, together with proposed large scale reorganisations in technical services and education. A number of strategic plans had been drawn up in what was regarded as key corporate areas (equivalent to key issues). These included:

Economic development strategy This was the strategic plan for the economic regeneration of the region covering the period 1991-94. The strategy provided a focus for all those working to improve the local economy. The strategy covered creating jobs and reducing unemployment, raising business and household incomes, ensuring that economic benefits are fairly distributed, ensuring sustainable economic development and an enhanced quality of life.

Transportation strategy The aim of this plan is to encourage people to use methods of transport other than the car and to make the alternatives available to car users more attractive. The policy aims to improve facilities for public transport, cycling and pedestrians, and to improve road safety by various means, particularly by enhanced use of traffic calming. The plan involves massive changes in spending capital resources available for transportation with the share allocated for roads building being reduced from 80 per cent to just over 30 per cent.

Environmental charter This is a broad statement of key environmental objectives and principles of the council. These include the promotion of sustainable development, the preservation of the natural environment, sustainable use of natural resources, increasing public awareness of environmental issues and to ensure that environmental implications of development are considered at all levels of council decision making.

Social strategy Social strategy addresses some of the key goals of the council in promoting economic and social well-being of communities, helping families, groups and organisations achieve their full potential, targeting services at individuals, groups and communities which are disadvantaged or have special needs, and encouraging active citizenship and development of caring communities.

Pre-fives strategy The purpose of this strategy is to increase the level of nursery and child care services, extending the degree of cooperation amongst the various sectors and extending the hours during which child care provision is available. A number of innovative schemes are planned including improved integration and coordination of services.

European strategy This strategy has the aim of enabling the people and businesses of the region to increase their understanding of the countries, peoples and institutions of Europe, and to gain the greatest possible social, cultural, environmental benefits from membership of the evolving European union, while also contributing to its further development.

Community safety strategy This strategy is concerned with safety at home, safety on the roads, safety from crime and the fear of crime, environmental safety, safety at work, school or college, consumer safety and safety to locate and invert.
  These strategies all link to service department plans or action plans and are delivered through them.

Implementation of the strategic plan In order to implement the strategic plan it will be necessary to develop a series of more detailed service and/or action plans relating to different parts of the strategy. Service planning will be discussed in the following section.

Service planning

We have seen that the strategic plan normally focuses on a limited number of key objectives that an authority may decide to pursue over a medium term period of three to four years. Strategic plans are normally drawn up at the corporate level. There is clearly, therefore, a need to operationalise these commitments and relate them to departments or sections that will actually deliver the service. This is done using *service plans* and *action plans*. Sometimes the service plan is called a business plan (usually by authorities who wish to distance themselves from their public service origins).

Service plans

These are normally developed for a given service and over a particular period of time and must at least reflect the priorities laid down by the strategic plan. Service plans would normally be updated annually. Given that strategic plans are corporately based and that service plans are departmentally based, then it is clear that some corporate issues will have implications for a number of service plans.

Action plans

These are short term plans (usually a year or even less). Generally they translate the service plan into specific actions for which named individuals are responsible. The action plans are valuable in ensuring that a service plan is actually implemented and in establishing appropriate accountability.

Service plans will generally facilitate linking the budget to the policy and performance review system since the resource implication of any development in the service plan should be made transparent.

Service position statement

Many authorities have attempted to facilitate their service planning process by summarising the current situation by means of position statements. One such authority is Newcastle Metropolitan Council. As an example we shall examine the service position statement for day care of children.

Case study: Newcastle Metropolitan Council

Position statement for day care for children

This is a summary of the most important elements of the statement.

Brief description of activity Consists of the provision of two pre-school playgroups, five day nurseries, and intermediate treatment centre for delinquent teenagers. Provides support for 70 voluntary pre-school playgroups and 250 childminders.

Revenue budget Total gross expenditure is £1,385,810 which is financed in different ways. In recent years the cost of this service has grown at a rate greater than the rate of inflation.

Reduction/growth agreed Reduced support for intermediate treatment facility and an increase in playgroup fees. However, the proposal for development of the under fives' service provided for in central contingencies has been implemented. A family centre has also been developed.

Staffing An overview of the staffing situation, broken down into different grades is provided.

Comparative position of the authority It was found that expenditure for 18 year olds by the city on these services is substantially above comparable authorities.

Efficiency/effectiveness studies These show that the authority has 70 per cent more children in care than the national average and expenditure under Section 1 of the Childcare Act is also much higher than average.

Client/user trends Preventative care facilities are provided for children at two pre- school playgroups, five day nurseries and an intermediate treatment centre.

Developing a service plan

In the previous section we discussed the use of a service position statement as a 'basic step' in establishing the service plan. A similar approach is the use of a technique called context analysis. Such an analysis requires consideration of a number of elements related to the way the service is provided and its potential for potential future changes, in terms of:

1   Resources.
2   Customers.
3   Suppliers. .
4   Competitors.
5   Partners.

We have discussed earlier the potential uses of PEST analysis in the strategic context in examining the external environment that an organisation is operating it. Clearly, the same kind of analysis but focused on the department or service unit perspective may still be useful at the service user level. Additionally, an internal analysis which focuses on organisational factions, management styles and methods, employees and personnel factors may also be useful.

SWOT analysis which are, we have seen, useful for identifying strengths and weaknesses at the organisational level, clearly, also has potential in the context of service plan development.

Service objectives

Service objectives require to be consistent with supporting the goals of the council but at this level require to be much more precise and specific. Service objectives may be of two types:

1   Service delivery objectives.
-       These will relate to service output.
2   Management objectives.
-       These relate to the development and management of the service.

The acronym SMART may be helpful in judging appropriate service objectives. SMART stands for:

Specific and concrete
Measurable
Achievable
Realistic
Timescale

If we examine the above:

Specific and concrete

An objective might be to widen the availability of nursery education. But a more specific objective might be 'to provide places for 95 per cent of four year olds over the next two years'.

Measurable

Instead of 'maintain street lighting to a good standard' to 'repair street lights within ten working days of notification'.

Achievable

Objectives need to be achievable and not simply a 'wish list'. For example there is little point in planning to clear a housing waiting list if there is absolutely no prospect of additional accommodation becoming available.

Realistic

Objectives should be realistic and indicate what level of resources are to be committed to achieve the objective, e.g. to offer two additional nursery classes each year by committing an additional £30,000.

Timescale

A reasonable timescale should be set e.g. 'all front line staff to undertake a customer care programme within the next 18 months'.

Case study: Kent County Council Social Services

Although this is termed a business plan it must be considered to be equivalent to a service plan.

The service plan is drawn up in the light of the corporate plan commitment which we have already seen earlier in the chapter. Amongst these is that to disadvantaged groups which states:

> top priority has been given to those in society with greatest needs. 1990-91 saw substantial investment in responding to children with special educational needs, improving childcare protection and accommodating the growing number of elderly, handicapped and mentally ill people requiring

care. 1991-92 and future years will see substantial new investment in this area.

The *service plan* contains a *departmental policy overview*. (This is rather more aggregated than the position statement of Newcastle Metropolitan Council described earlier.) This overview recognises that in 1992-93 the department will spend £149 million, help over 30,000 people and employ over 6,000 people. It mentions the department's link with other agencies in the delivery of services including health authorities, district councils and the private and voluntary sectors. Services are provided by staff from the five social services areas which are largely conterminous with the existing health authority boundaries.

There is a *review of external pressure and trends* (similar to a PEST analysis). The main parts of this are:

1   A continuous increase in the number of child protection referrals and registrations.
2   A growing number of highly dependent elderly people, especially over the age of 75 with a high incidence of dementia.
3   The implementation of the NHS and Community Care Act from 1st April 1993 which makes social services departments the lead agency for community care.
4   Implementation of the Childrens' Act.
5   Pressures to reduce overheads and management costs but also to improve financial, personnel and management reports as part of the devolved management strategy.

The department has established clear service objectives and performance targets and indicators. Space does not allow us to cover all of these but those for *children and families* are as follows: (Table 2.3)

Table 2.3
Objectives, indicators and targets

	Policy objective	Indicator	Target value (current year's target in brackets)
1	Minimise no. of children entering care	No. entering care per 1000 population under 18 years	1.7 (1.7)
2	To minimise length of stay in care	Average length of stay in care	20 months (21 months)
3	To increase the proportion in care who are placed with substitute families	% of children in care placed with substitute families in year	72% (70%)
4	To increase the proportion of children in care placed for adoption	% of children in care placed for adoption in year	6% (6%)
5	To protect children currently at risk of abuse	Ratio of new registrations to deregistrations	1 to 1.1 (1 to 1.1)

The service plan also outlines a series of responses given the above objectives, the external pressures and trends and the available funding. These responses include:

1   Responding to child protection referrals, ensuring that all cases are dealt with by qualified social workers.
2   Partnership with other public, private and voluntary sectors in a mixed economy of welfare provision.
3   Providing an increased number of packages of care to meet individual requirements through care management, ensuring growth of user involvement and choice and targeting of services on the most dependent.
4   Providing more linked service care for elderly people including 24 hour support for their carers.
5   Provide wide support for children leaving care and a wide range of preventative services for children and their families.

6   Maximising the use of technology to improve the flow of information and to enhance service quality and effectiveness.

7   Continue to streamline management structures and reduce overhead as a proportion of direct services cost.

In order that the plan can be implemented the detailed implications for particular area offices are spelled out. For example, for services for children and families in the Canterbury and Thanet area:

1   Reducing the number of children placed in private and voluntary residential care arrangements from 56 to 35.

2   Placing 317 children in foster homes at an average weekly cost of £182.70.

3   As a result of the Criminal Justice Act the number of children placed in secure accommodation is likely to rise from 8 to 15 with associated financial consequences.

4   Overall it is planned that during the course of the year the number of children looked after should reduce to 420 and that 30 children should be placed for adoption in the course of the year.

Summary

In this chapter we have given a brief outline of the strategic and service planning processes within which performance review systems are likely to operate. We shall proceed in the next chapters to consider issues specifically related to performance review.

3   Performance indicators

Introduction

In the first Chapter we considered the background to performance review and the political and managerial environments within which performance review systems are developed. In the second Chapter we reviewed the strategic planning and service planning systems to which performance review systems may relate. This is highly significant since if an authority or 'service' cannot decide what it is trying to achieve, i.e. what performance is all about, then there is little point in reviewing its achievement.

In the performance review field, however, there is considerable ambiguity and uncertainty about definitions. We plan to clarify some of these matters in this Chapter and to outline some of the suggested approaches to the development of performance review in the following one.

Definitions

Many commentators have suggested that performance review has three related elements: economy, efficiency and effectiveness.

Butt and Palmer (1985) give the following definitions:

Economy

The practice by management of the virtues of thrift and good housekeeping. An economical operation acquires resources in appropriate quality and quantity at the lowest cost.

Efficiency

Making sure that the maximum useful output is gained from the resources devoted to each activity, or, alternatively, that only the minimum level of resources are devoted to achieving a given level of output. An operation could be said to have increased in efficiency if either lower costs were used to produce a given amount of output, or a given level of cost resulted in increased output.

Effectiveness

Ensuring that the output from any given activity (or the impact that services have on a community) is achieving the desired results. To evaluate effectiveness we need to establish that approved/desired goals are being achieved. A goal (or operating objective) may be defined as a concrete expression of a policy objective. This is not necessarily a straightforward procedure; some goals may not be initially apparent. Once a set of goals has been established we need to determine whether these goals are being accomplished.
(Butt and Palmer, 1985, pp10-11)

Clearly, the concept of effectiveness is very important since there is little point in acquiring resources inexpensively and being good at turning inputs into outputs, if at the end of the day, the outputs are not really the ones desired or they do not have appropriate impacts on the community. The concept of effectiveness links performance review to the political objectives of the council. A succinct outline of the difference between efficiency and effectiveness is that effectiveness is 'doing the right thing', whilst efficiency is 'doing the thing right'.

Given the social remit of local authorities it is not surprising that there has been pressure for inclusion of equity in the performance review framework (see for example Flynn, 1993).

In our visit to Bristol City Council we found that they had not only added equity to their performance review framework but two further E's: empowerment and the environment.

Jackson and Palmer (1992) have also proposed the addition of excellence, entrepreneurship, expertise and electability and possibly Europe and the environment.

The extended VFM framework which incorporates equity, entrepreneurship, excellence, expertise and electability by adding them to economy, efficiency and effectiveness brings the issues of performance measurement much closer to the reality of management problems. There are many different dimensions to performance and the problem which faces management is to choose the appropriate trade offs between each of the elements.
(Jackson and Palmer, 1992, p20)

Pollitt has similarly argued that 'the alphabet of performance does not begin and end with the 3Es' (1986, p161) and he cites a number of other criteria which have been suggested as relevant including availability, awareness, extensiveness and acceptability.

Measuring performance

Having clarified what may be involved in measuring performance we now require to develop appropriate measurement tools.

In assessing performance, *performance indicators* and *measures* are generally used. Jackson and Palmer attempt to distinguish the difference between these two terms.

> A distinction is often made between performance *measures* and performance *indicators*. Where economy, efficiency and effectiveness can be measured precisely and unambiguously it is usual to talk about performance measures. However, when as is most usually the case it is not possible to obtain a precise measure it is usual to refer to performance indicators.
> (Jackson and Palmer, 1989, p2)

There are perhaps a limited number of situations in local government where precise measures can be derived. An example might be where a precise definition of water quality had been established and precise measurements are taken to review performance against standard.

Where such measures are unavailable then indicators have to be employed. There is much discussion of indicators in the literature but few attempts to establish appropriate definitions. One attempt at defining the key property of performance indicators was made by Cuenin (1987) (in the Higher Education Field).

> When an indicator shows a difference in one direction this means that the situation is better whereas if it shows a difference in the opposite direction this means that the situation is less favourable.
> (Cuenin, 1987, p118)

This helps to distinguish performance indicators from the large amount of other management data which although interesting and relevant, may not give any insight into performance issues. This latter kind of information can be designated a *management statistic*. Failure to distinguish between the two can lead to a situation described by Elton (1987) in which:

Anything that can be easily measured becomes a performance indicator. (Elton, 1987, p12)

Dochy and Segers (1990) propose a number of other desirable properties of performance indicators (PIS):

A first requirement is that they (PI's) should be clearly related to the defined function of the institution. A second requirement is that they are only what their name states - indicators of the extent to which institutional goals are achieved. A third requirement is that they should be a valid operationalisation of what they intend to indicate and that they can be measured and interpreted in this way.
(Dochy & Segers,1990, p3)

Jackson (1998) also supplies a list of desirable properties of indicators:

Consistency

The definitions used to produce the indicators should be consistent over time and between units.

Comparability

Following from consistency, it is only reasonable to compare like with like.

Clarity

Performance indices should be simple, well defined and easily understood.

Controllability

The manager's performance should only be measured for those areas that (s)he has control over.

Contingency

Performance is not independent of the environment within which decisions are made; which includes the organisation structure, the management style adopted as well as the uncertainty and complexity of the external environment.

Comprehensive

Do the indicators reflect those aspects of behaviour which are important to management decision makers?

Bounded

Concentrate upon a limited number of key indices of performance - those which are likely to give the biggest pay off.

Relevance

Many applications require specific performance indicators relevant to their special needs and conditions. Do the indicators service these needs?

Feasibility

Are the targets based on unrealistic expectations? Can the targets be reached through reasonable actions?
(Jackson, 1988, p12)

Examples of indicators

We shall now consider a number of examples of performance indicators that could be used in practical situations.

For example performance indicators related to *economy* might be:

1   Cost per nursery place provided.
2   Cost per planning application processed.

A practical example of a performance indicator for economy could be Bristol City Council's indicator for ensuring that the number and average value of response repairs is not more than 5% more than the previous year.

Another economy indicator used by the same authority in housing service for special needs is the average cost of warden services compared with the previous years.

It is suggested by the Service Planning Guide, Central Regional Council (1993) that efficiency can be measured in 6 different ways. This is in fact based on earlier Audit Commission guidelines.

1   Utilisation measures.
2   Productivity.

3   Response times.
4   Task completed.
5   Restricted services.
6   Volume of work.

Utilisation measures

Measure the extent to which available resources are used (expressed as a percentage). For example, Wyre District Council in attempting to measure provision of adequate car parking spaces, use the occupancy rate of parking spaces throughout the year and the demand for additional places.

Brent use ratios of pupil numbers to pupil capacity in secondary schools. This authority also use the percentage downtime of different computer systems as a measure of their utilisation.

Productivity

Is the amount of useful work carried out by employees in a defined length of time. For example Kent uses the proportion of clients receiving community care whose service plans were up to date by the end of the year as a measure of efficiency.

Response times

This represents the time taken to respond to a request for service. For example Brent use the % response repairs undertaken within specific periods for different priority categories - category (1(a) = 24 hours, 1(b) = 3 days, 2 - 25 days).

Task completed

This corresponds to the completion of a particular task. For example, Wyre District Council in looking at environmental protection and enhancement use the number of new enforcement cases concluded and received in the last month as a measure of the efficiency of its enforcement procedures.

One of Brent's PI's for environmental health is the number of blocks in Chalkhill successfully treated for cockroaches!

Restricted service

This is used for measurement where service provision is restricted and unlikely to meet project needs.

This can be used to measure whether a service is utilised by its target population.

For example, Central Regional Council used uptake of childcare places provided in the Raploch area by families resident in the area as a performance indicator. This is because Raploch is a deprived community and it is a policy target to ensure that its residents do in fact enjoy available services.

Kent County Council also has an indicator which falls into this category. In the context of their residential service it uses the proportion of clients in Kent residential care falling into various dependency bands as an indicator.

Volume of service

This measure of efficiency corresponds to the volume or throughput of work within a service. For example, an indicator for a Communications Department might use the number of press releases completed.

Bristol City Council in its control of unsatisfactory housing services, uses as an indicator the number of inspections of hostels compared with the previous years.

Effectiveness

As we have seen, effectiveness is about providing the right services to allow the authority to implement its policies and objectives. Examples of effectiveness indicators might be the extent to which users are satisfied with the service (which might be measured by survey results, levels of demand for a service and levels of complaints received). This might also be tackled by looking at the way that user needs had been met.

For example Kent use figures for user satisfaction to evaluate the performance of its Social Services. It has adopted the percentage of adult service users who, according to their surveys, rank the service as satisfactory as an indicator of effectiveness.

Brent has used the number of formal complaints received in a period as a standard performance indicator for each service. A formal complaint is one that cannot be resolved at the point where the service is provided (normally with the line manager). Formal complaints are then taken up with the relevant service director.

Equality indicators

Examples of the use of equality indicators are presented by Jones (1995). These all relate to work in the London Borough of Hackney. This paper refers to three classes of equality indicators. These are:

1   *Access equality indicators* which include indicators on access to buildings and availability of translators.

2   *Staffing equality indicators* in which indicators are provided on staffing composition, and disability/age profile in comparison to the community as a whole.

3   *Service delivery equality indicators* - these particularly focus on service usage and take up in relation to gender, race, age and disability.

It may be the case that too many authorities have devoted their efforts to developing indicators for economy and efficiency to the detriment of efforts to develop appropriate indicators for effectiveness. Butt and Palmer also comment on the difficulty of developing appropriate measures for effectiveness. However, the Audit Commission (1989), not impressed by what it perceived to be inertia, proposed that:

> The commission, therefore, believes that it does a dis-service to local Government to dwell too much on theoretical difficulties in measuring performance.
> (Audit Commission, 1989, p4)

Use (and misuse) of performance indicators

Unlike performance measures, indicators do not give a precise and unambiguous view of the situation. To quote Jackson and Palmer (1989, p2): 'performance indicators are provocative and suggestive, they alert managers to the need to examine the issue further'.

This view is supported by Carter (1991) who likens the use of indicators to tin openers:

> Indicators are simply descriptive. They do not speak for themselves. They may signal that a particular unit be it a Crown Court, prison or bank is a statistical outlier, but no conclusion can be drawn from this fact in itself. It is simply an invitation to investigate, to probe and to ask questions.
> (Carter, 1991, p94)

For example, a housing department could have an indicator showing a high rate of voids which might compare unfavourably with neighbouring authorities. This might indicate a lack of managerial efficiency on behalf of the housing department. On the other hand, a comparatively high void rate might be related to the existence of a higher than average proportion of hard-to-let properties or a high proportion of properties that required considerable maintenance work when the property turns-over.

Again, a school might perform relatively poorly on an indicator related to examination results. Since, however, it is well known that examination performance is closely related to socio-economic class, it will be important to take proper account of the social background of the school intake before rushing to any hasty judgement about the performance of the school.

These examples illustrate the importance of using appropriate managerial judgement in interpreting performance indicators and not using them in a mechanistic or automatic way. To quote the Committee of Vice chancellors and Principals (CVCP) (1986) in the Higher Education Field:

> The use of PI's is an aid to good judgement and not a substitute for it. The numbers will not and never can 'speak for themselves'. Mere inspection is not enough - interpretation is always necessary. It cannot be assumed that even a wide variation from a single indicator is either desirable or undesirable.

There are, of course, many other ways to misuse indicators in addition to failing to provide appropriate managerial judgement. We have already discussed the need for indicators to be properly related to objectives, otherwise service may be judged on a whole series of unrelated and contradictory indicators. Indicators may also be *data driven* ie. derived because the data exists, not because it provides a particularly meaningful indicator of performance. It is also extremely demotivating if the indicator is unduly affected by outside factors over which those evaluated have no effective control. Obviously in this situation we cannot expect the organisation to take ownership of its performance. An example of this is the practice of using crime statistics to judge the performance of the police. It's perhaps not surprising that senior police offices tend to believe that such indicators reflect the performance of society as a whole rather than that of the police.

Summary

Having reviewed the development and use of performance indicators we shall now review the performance review systems in which such indicators are likely to be employed.

4   Performance review systems

Introduction

As we have seen in the previous chapter, while much has been written about performance indicators, relatively little has been published on performance review systems. Within this chapter we shall survey approaches suggested by the Audit and Accounts Commission and other authors before proceeding in subsequent chapters to comment on the results of our own research in this area.

Audit Commission's approach to performance review

Ball and Monaghan have observed that 'the Audit Commission has championed the performance review cause' (1993, p38) and whilst other commentators have also promoted its introduction and compiled accompanying 'how to do it' guides (for example, Butt and Palmer, 1985; Jackson and Palmer, 1989); the high profile which the Audit Commission has within the local government sphere has given its advocacy and recommended approach predominance.

Throughout the 1980s, the Audit Commission produced a series of publications, *Performance review in local government - a handbook for auditors and local authorities*, which were updated and refined in the light of accumulated experience and the changing circumstances of local government. In the 1988 handbook, it was proposed that performance review should underpin the management process shown in Figure 4.1.

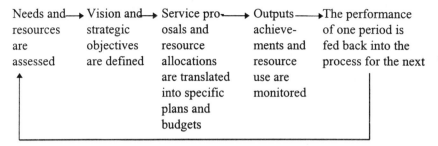

Figure 4.1   The Audit Commission's management process
(Audit Commission, 1989, p2)

In December 1989, The Commission published *Managing services effectively - performance review,* which was a refined and modified version of the approach espoused in the earlier handbooks. Following this publication, the Commission's attention in the performance domain was dominated by preparation for and implementation of the Citizen's Charter and thus despite all the reforms which have occurred in the local government arena since 1989 and the experience accumulated by authorities operating performance review systems, the Audit Commission's approach to performance review remains unchanged to date. It has recently published a series of papers which emphasise the role of the individual in determining overall organisational performance and indicating methods of strengthening this (Audit Commission 1995a, 1995b, 1995c) but the Commission has not updated its recommended performance review approach.

Given the profile and standing which the Commission has, it is highly probable that its recommended approach to performance review will significantly influence how local authorities embark on reviewing their performance. Consequently, the process advocated by the Audit Commission will be considered in detail. In the 1989 paper, the Commission proposed that a council intending to strengthen its performance review capability needs to focus on four main steps which are separately considered in detail below:

1   Measuring performance.
2   Assessing quality and effectiveness.
3   Monitoring and reporting performance.
4   Making it happen.

Measuring performance

The Commission considers that performance review ultimately depends on 'defining what performance means, and then measuring it'. It is considered that most services or activities can be (or ought to be) measured along four dimensions:

1   The cost.

2   The resources provided - for example the staff, buildings and other resources employed in providing swimming pools or residential homes for the elderly. It is sometimes possible also to measure the units of service that these resources jointly provide, for example the number of residential places.

3   The outputs - the use made of these resources, or the service actually delivered to the public, for example the number of residents in council homes, or the number of swimmers.

4   The outcomes - the ultimate value or benefit of the service to its users. Examination results, for example, provide one measure of the outcome of secondary schooling.

These measures are considered 'to provide the raw materials for performance review' but that they normally only come to life in the form of performance indicators relating to economy, efficiency and effectiveness (see chapter 3). These indicators can then be monitored over time or compared with targets or with performance elsewhere.

The Commission also considers that it is important that the target population for each service is defined and measured, thus providing the basis for two further performance indicators:

1   Level of Service - for example, the number of places provided per elderly resident, or the number of leisure facilities in relation to the catchment population.

2   Take-up - for example, the proportion of the catchment population that use the swimming pool - often useful as a proxy indicator of the quality of the facilities provided.

It is argued that:

> Once these performance indicators have been identified and measured, then the performance of the service can be monitored and compared with the expected levels of achievement. Problems and opportunities can be spotted and investigated and corrective action initiated where needed. (1989, p3)

However, the Commission recognises that practice is not always as easy as 'the theory of performance measurement' and considers measuring 'service outcome' or effectiveness to be a particularly significant difficulty. It is conceded that it is usually easier to measure the 'output' of a service, with the number of children educated by a school cited as an example, but it is proposed that such measures are of little value 'unless there is reasonable reassurance about the effectiveness and quality of the service'. It is proposed that measuring inputs seldom presents difficulties but that this potentially creates the problem of 'the measurable driving out the immeasurable' with performance review consequently being biased towards 'reducing cost rather than improving effectiveness'. The literature which underlines such difficulties is acknowledged but it is argued that whilst 'respecting the quality of these arguments, the Commission believes it is wrong to conclude that performance measurement is quite so difficult and dangerous'. In particular, it is considered better to 'have incomplete or imperfect measures of performance than none at all'. Furthermore, the Commission argues that many of the objections assume that the audience for performance measures 'has no judgement or common-sense' whereas in fact they will normally know the limitations and pitfalls of the information and are well capable of determining what conclusions can and cannot be drawn. It is concluded:

> The Commission therefore believes that it is a dis-service to local government to dwell too much on the theoretical difficulties of measuring performance. What is more useful is to propose practical ways in which local authorities actually can measure their performance, while avoiding the worst consequences of misleading indicators.
> (1989, p4)

The paper then proceeds to advise authorities on specific aspects of measuring cost, resource inputs, outputs and outcomes but an underlying theme is the reiteration that the measures are only of significance if service quality and effectiveness are not ignored and it is considered that this is one of the main areas in which performance review systems can be improved.

Evaluating quality and effectiveness

The Commission proposes that:

> No matter what a service costs, or how generously it is provided, the most critical indicator of its performance is the value or benefit that it confers on its users. Simply measuring costs and quantities with no regard for quality, is not a satisfactory basis for performance review. At the same time once a council has some assurance about service quality, it can then attach more importance to other measures such as unit costs, making the whole performance review process more credible.
> (1989, p6)

The Commission on a number of occasions in this paper use quality and effectiveness interchangeably proposing at one point that 'the effectiveness or impact of most services can reasonably be gauged by inspecting and controlling the quality of the service itself in relation to accepted standards'. This point is somewhat contentious since quality and effectiveness can reasonably be argued to be different things. There are a range of definitions of service quality. One of the most commonly used is that from Zeithaml et al (1992) who define service quality as the extent to which the service meets user expectation. Effectiveness, on the other hand, relates to policy achievement. It can thus be seen that, although closely related (policy aims will often be fulfilled when the service meets user expectations), they are not necessarily the same thing.

The Commission proposes that the simplest solution to the difficult issue of assessing effectiveness and quality, is to use proxy measures of impact. The following example is given:

> One of the reasons for providing recreation centres may be to occupy teenagers and so reduce vandalism. This impact may be hard to measure directly, but a fair proxy is simply the number of teenagers - or particular types of teenagers - that actually use the facilities.
> (1989, p6)

One might reasonably suggest that concurrent monitoring of vandalism levels would significantly strengthen this proxy measure of effectiveness. It is also suggested that a simple proxy measure for many services is 'the level of public complaints, or the level of customer demand and customer retention'. It is proposed that service users should be the judges of the quality of the service and it is suggested that 'surveys of users, recording their opinion of the current service, and their suggestions for what else might be provided' should help gauge quality and identify the main opportunities for improvement. It is also proposed that quality control and quality assurance systems will have a significant role in improving service quality and effectiveness.

Whilst it would be difficult to argue with the logic of the foregoing, it must be observed that throughout the 28 paragraphs devoted to the evaluation of quality and effectiveness, no mention is made of policies, members or politics despite the fact that the effectiveness of a service must be related to what policy objectives are being pursued by a local authority. The entire discussion is devoid of any policy dimension or recognition of the political process underpinning the delivery of services by local councils. Whilst this is the case throughout the publication, the omission seems particularly acute when the effectiveness of services is being considered. There is also no acknowledgement that a trade-off normally exists between service quality and the cost of provision and that often a policy decision is taken as to the quality of service a council can 'afford'.

Monitoring and reporting performance

The Commission proposes that there are four main steps to developing an effective monitoring and reporting system:

1   Identify the key issues for each service, and the key processes that genuinely need to be monitored; and select the performance indicators that measure them.

2   Clarify responsibilities for monitoring performance - who needs to monitor what, and how often, particularly members, senior management, and the front line managers of each service.

3   Set targets or yardsticks, including quality objectives that indicate whether performance is good or bad, or at least getting better or worse.

4   Design and produce the appropriate reports.
     (1989, p9)

In identifying key performance indicators, it is stressed that monitoring performance is not simply a matter of 'scanning whatever statistics happen to come to hand' but rather there needs to be a focus on key issues and it is considered that these will depend to some extent 'upon the audience, the time period and local circumstances'. It is also proposed that:

> In choosing the critical indicators, it is often useful to make a distinction between operational performance, that needs to be monitored at regular intervals, and underlying performance (for example quality and effectiveness) that may be just as critical, but which it is not sensible to debate every month, even if the information were available.
> (1989, p9)

In clarifying monitoring responsibilities, the Audit Commission proposes that the purpose, type and frequency of reporting data can be summarised as a series of pyramids as shown in figure 4.2 overleaf.

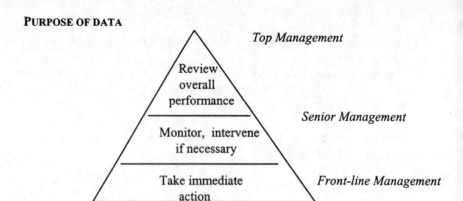

PURPOSE OF DATA

Top Management

Review overall performance

Senior Management

Monitor, intervene if necessary

Take immediate action

Front-line Management

TYPE OF DATA

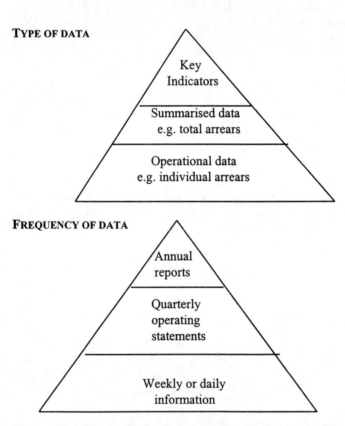

Key Indicators

Summarised data e.g. total arrears

Operational data e.g. individual arrears

FREQUENCY OF DATA

Annual reports

Quarterly operating statements

Weekly or daily information

Figure 4.2   The Audit Commission's monitoring pyramids
(Audit Commission, 1989, p11)

It is recognised that members should be involved in the monitoring of performance as well as management but because they 'cannot possibly monitor every aspect of every service at every meeting' the Commission proposes that:

1   Members regularly monitor a limited set of measures that they judge to be most critical, supplemented with an annual review of the whole service.
2   They ensure that officers are adequately monitoring everything else, at the appropriate detail and frequency.
3   They require any deviations beyond a certain level of significance to be reported to them immediately.
     (1989, pp10-11)

Additionally, it is considered that councils have an obligation to report performance to the public normally through broad annual reports and that information is increasingly being demanded by service users about standards.

The Commission asserts that performance indicators are pointless without associated targets or yardsticks and considers that:

> As a general rule, any performance indicator that a council monitors should have some kind of comparative figure set beside it. There are two possible approaches: setting targets, or using comparisons such as last year's figures or averages for other authorities.
> (1989, p12)

The Commission produced a data supplement to the 1988 *Performance Review in Local Government* handbook comprising a large number of benchmark figures and it is proposed that councils should compare their performance with these national average and good practice targets and report performance accordingly.

The final stage of monitoring and reporting performance is designing and producing the appropriate reports. It is proposed that the following questions should be asked in deciding what information and comparative indicators are to be included in any monitoring report:

1   Whom is the report for, and for what activities are they responsible?
2   What decisions do they have to take, or genuinely need to monitor, in the sense that they might intervene if the results were unsatisfactory?
3   How frequently do these decisions need to be taken?

The report should then contain the minimum information needed to satisfy these requirements. Authorities are urged to make sure that reports are well presented and to observe the following points:

1   Avoid over-crowding the page.
2   Use clear headings.

3   Employ graphs to illustrate trends and variations.

4   Highlight the key figures.

5   Include text commentary alongside the relevant figures.

Authorities are reminded that reporting and monitoring should not be confined to quantifiable performance indicators and it is proposed that issues such as quality and effectiveness should have a regular place on the agendas of members and senior management perhaps at an annual meeting devoted to performance review.

Making it happen

The Commission proposes that setting up a performance review system is relatively easy but that the best defined systems will serve little purpose unless members and officers take them seriously. Whilst the latter point is undoubtedly true, the assertion that establishing a system is comparatively easy is more dubious and it is intended in this book to analyse the process of constructing a review process and to assess how easy it really is. The Commission considers that:

> It is also easy to go through the motions of monitoring and reporting performance, without taking it seriously - avoiding the sensitive issues, or the awkward comparisons, turning a blind eye to obvious weaknesses, and focusing on why things cannot be changed rather than how they could be. (1989, p16)

It is proposed that to counteract this, a conscious and concerted effort needs to be made in the following areas:

1   Ensure that each department has adequate arrangements for performance review.

2   Make the chief executive responsible for the process, and provide him or her with staff resources.

3   Involve members.
     (1989, p16)

It is suggested that there are three main preconditions for effective performance review in a department namely, an accountable management structure, a clear commitment to quality, and leadership from the top. In terms of chief executive involvement, it is considered that he or she should not simply 'occupy the top of the performance review pyramid' but should in fact have responsibility (and the corresponding authority) for the way in which the system operates. In particular:

1   Ensuring that each department has an effective performance review system.
2   Monitoring key aspects of each department's performance, reviewing results with its chief officer and where possible agreeing corrective action.
3   Organising the council's top level performance review system - in particular providing regular monitoring information to its central policy-making committee.
4   Recommend which services or activities should be subjected to an in-depth review of performance; agreeing the arrangements for doing this with the appropriate chief officer; and reviewing departments' progress in implementing agreed changes.
    (1989, p17)

In addition to chief executive input, the Commission considers that effective performance review will almost certainly require 'the assistance of a small central staff, respected by service departments and well-managed by central chief officers and members'. It is asserted that these staff will report to the chief executive and will be responsible for both performance review and policy planning. It is proposed that it is not the job of such central staff to directly review department's performance but rather to act as catalyst for the efforts of others by:

1   Helping departments design and improve their performance review systems, and promoting a reasonably uniform approach across all departments.
2   Designing and operating the central policy review process.
3   Helping the chief executive to identify the issues to bring to the attention of the centre, or to raise with other chief officers.
4   Taking part or leading in-depth reviews of services whose performance appears to need improvement.
    (1989, p18)

It is recognised that the exact arrangements will vary from council to council and that smaller authorities will not be able to employ the same number of staff as large councils but it is suggested that in such instances, the chief executive could second some of his departmental staff on a part time basis.

In terms of involving members, the Commission asserts that:

Performance review should form an integral part of each member's work for the council, in the same way as it forms an integral part of a manager's job. In general therefore the Commission believes that performance review should not be hived off to a separate performance review committee. Temporary working parties can deal with particular issues, and there may be a case for a special group of members to oversee the working of the

performance review system itself. But the actual responsibility for reviewing performance should rest with the same committees who are already responsible for each service.
(1989, p18)

It is considered that the change needed is simply to give performance review the proper weight in the agenda and business of committees, probably at the expense of detailed involvement in the day to day operations of the service. It is suggested that members should receive operations reports from officers as the first substantive item on the committee agenda and that once a year, committees might hold a special meeting solely devoted to the review of the year's performance. It is also proposed that members have the task of ensuring that performance review is linked to the strategic planning process but it is not indicated how such a linkage might be achieved. The Commission also suggests that member-officer reviews might prove a useful vehicle for reviewing performance and that above all 'there is little point in monitoring performance and identifying short comings unless something is done'.

The Audit Commission concludes this guide to performance review by providing some advice to councils embarking on setting up a system:

> The first requirement is that the initiative must be taken seriously, and not simply regarded as one more management drill. The objective is not to go through the motions, but to highlight genuine problems and to secure improvement and change. It should have visible and sustained backing from members, from the chief executive and from chief officers. And this backing should be demonstrated by action rather than simply by words, and by the use made of the results.
> (1989, p19)

It is suggested that councils developing a system can do so in 'easy stages' and that they should work from the front-line upwards, start with the most promising areas, and avoid being too ambitious. The Audit Commission does, however, suggest that the majority of councils already have some elements of a performance review system in place but need to develop these into something that is more systematic and effective.

Throughout *Managing services effectively - performance review*, the Audit Commission's approach is asserted as the definitive process. There is no suggestion that alternative processes or mechanisms for reviewing performance may exist or indeed be better suited to a particular local authority's needs and circumstances. The approach is postulated as best practice but without any substantiation being given. Nor is it apparent that the Audit Commission's suggested approach has actually been tested in the complex, turbulent and political environment which characterises most local authorities.

Unlike the previous Audit Commission publications on this subject, there is no discussion of how performance review might fit into the overall management and political framework of a local council. Passing reference is made to the need for a link to exist between reviewing performance and the authority's planning process, but despite the fact that detailed guidance is given on significantly less imperative matters such as the presentation of performance reports, this particular issue is skipped over without any useful advice being offered. Overall, the policy dimension of performance and local government more generally, is virtually ignored particularly in the discussion of service effectiveness.

In subsequent chapters, the approaches to performance review actually adopted by local authorities will be examined and these can then be compared with the Audit Commission's espoused process. However, there are a number of other mechanisms which have been advocated in the public domain.

The Accounts Commission's approach to performance review

Being north of the border, the Accounts Commission has had nothing like the impact or profile which the Audit Commission has and, prior to local Government reorganisation in 1996, encompassed only 65 local authorities as compared with the 449 which the Audit Commission had under its wing. Its approach is consequently different and it has tended to work wherever possible in partnership with local authorities. Indeed the Accounts Commission set up a value for money liaison group with the Convention of Scottish Local Authorities to determine the most appropriate methods of pursuing value for money within Scottish local government.

The management practices which the Accounts Commission intimated a local authority should have in place if the necessary arrangements for securing economy, efficiency and effectiveness are likely to exist included 'regular monitoring of results against predetermined and quantified performance objectives and standards' (Accounts Commission, 1988b). In examining an authority's value for money arrangements, auditors were advised to focus on a number of areas including the 'existence of commitment and a corporate approach to value for money within an authority, for example, steering group or performance review machinery'. In a subsequent publication, the Accounts Commission outlined how performance review might operate within the total framework of a council's operations as reproduced in figure 4.3. This indicates the need for reviewing both the performance of operational activities and policies and suggests that performance should be related to targets and that the actual results achieved should lead to replanning at the strategic level.

In developing this further, the Accounts Commission published research in 1992 which had been undertaken in collaboration with the Institute of Housing in Scotland examining current management practice and progress made towards

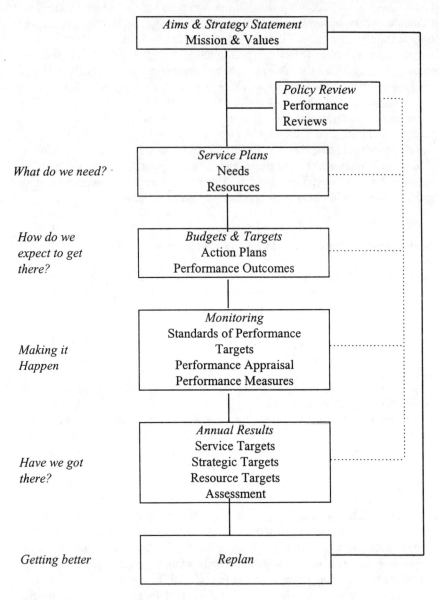

Figure 4.3   Accounts Commission's framework of council operations
(Accounts Commission, 1992a, p13)

establishing a performance culture within the housing area (Accounts Commission, 1992b). It was reported that:

> Just over half (57%) of the authorities have either a policy commitment to introduce performance review or have some system in operation. Only a few authorities, however, have developed a systematic approach to performance review of the majority of housing functions.
> (Accounts Commission, 1992b, p11)

A number of case studies were conducted within this research programme and it was indicated that amongst the case authorities:

1   The development of performance review is not dependent on one organisational form and can operate in a centralised or decentralised structure.
2   Performance review, with effective use of information technology and trained staff, can be operated successfully in authorities irrespective of size.
3   Performance review is relevant and applicable to all types of housing agency.
    (Accounts Commission, 1992b, p13)

Some advice on developing good practice in performance management was then offered including clarification of the relationship between objectives as outlined in figure 4.4. It was suggested that:

> The strategic objectives and indicators defined by authorities should provide senior management and the administration with a clear view of departmental performance. Below this level, however, authorities should ensure that key objectives and indicators for individual functions are established for each organisational level. Authorities can then monitor trends and variations in performance at different operational and management levels, identify more accurately the source of difficulties, and set targets which increase accountability for performance throughout the department.
> (Accounts Commission, 1992b, pp14-15)

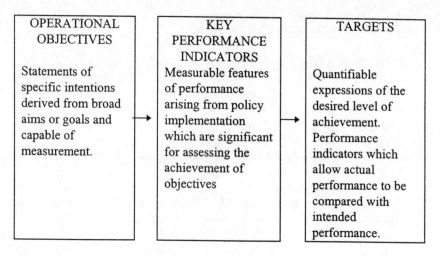

OPERATIONAL OBJECTIVES	KEY PERFORMANCE INDICATORS	TARGETS
Statements of specific intentions derived from broad aims or goals and capable of measurement.	Measurable features of performance arising from policy implementation which are significant for assessing the achievement of objectives	Quantifiable expressions of the desired level of achievement. Performance indicators which allow actual performance to be compared with intended performance.

Figure 4.4   Relationship between objectives, indicators and targets
(Accounts Commission, 1992b, p14)

The report strongly argues that the development of effective performance management also requires adequate costing of the management and administration of delivering individual housing functions:

> By establishing cost centres for individual housing functions, accompanied by key operational objectives, indicators and targets at different organisational levels, an integrated performance review framework can be operated throughout the annual cycle of activity.
> (Accounts Commission, 1992b, p15)

It was proposed that 'performance budgeting and performance review are essential elements of an effective management process' (1992b, p16). Figure 4.5 sets out their inter-relationship in a housing service as perceived by the Accounts Commission. The report concludes by providing a framework for improving housing performance as indicated in Figure 4.6. Whilst the analysis from which these recommendations emerged was concerned with housing, the findings are of wider applicability.

The Accounts Commission approach highlights a number of issues in the performance review domain not apparent in the Audit Commission discourse. In addition to being considerably less paternalistic, the Accounts Commission highlights the need to integrate the performance review process into the overall management of the authority and in particular recognises that a policy dimension exists in local government and thus that performance in relation to policy achievements needs to be considered within a performance review system. The need for a link to be established with the budgetary process is also indicated and

76

it is suggested that cost centres with clear operational objectives and associated performance indicators, which have cascaded down form the organisation's overall strategy, may be an appropriate means of achieving this. For the performance indicators, the accent is on comparing performance against pre-set internal targets rather than external criteria such as the Audit Commission's benchmark figures or average performance levels for local authorities. Little attention however, is paid to non-quantifiable performance and in particular there is an inadequate treatment of service quality. Within the Accounts Commission dialogue, the emphasis is on promoting change as opposed to the Audit Commission's work which smacks of 'imposing' change.

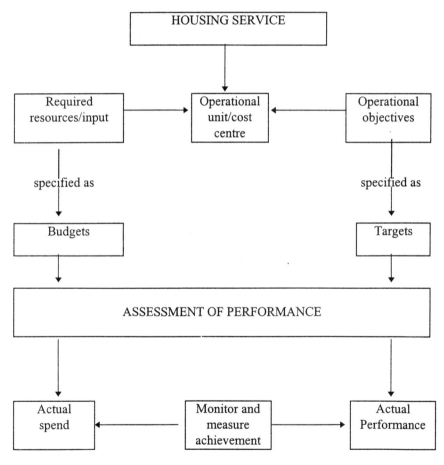

Figure 4.5   Integrated performance budgeting - performance review framework

(Accounts Commission, 1992b, p15)

ASSESS CURRENT POSITION	* Are derived objectives stated and linked to standards, indicators & targets? * Is performance measured? * Are service management costs and outputs measured?
PROMOTE CHANGE	* Motivate staff to believe in performance, quality services and accountability. * Develop and train staff in performance concepts and practice. * Support members to develop strategic monitoring role.
DEVOLVE AUTHORITY AND ACCOUNT-ABILITY	* Devolve responsibility for resources and staff. * Give authority for decision-making to lowest appropriate level. * Establish accountability for performance.
DEVELOP INFORMATION TECHNOLOGY	* Train management staff to understand/use IT effectively for performance review. * Specify management information requirements. * Design systems for flexibility and change.
ADDRESS QUALITY	* Specify standards of service to be achieved. * Document procedures. * Develop tenant/consumer perspectives of quality.
PLAN PERFORMANCE REVIEW	* Set measurable objectives, indicators, targets for each function. * Define organisational/officer levels at which performance will be reviewed. * Establish monitoring cycle for each organisational level.
ESTABLISH COSTS	* Disaggregate functions to individual cost centres. * Identify cost components for each cost centres. * Set cost centre target.
MEASURE PERFORMANCE AND COSTS	* Measure outputs/outcomes against costs and resources. * Measure each function at district and local level. * Measure quality via consumer feedback and internally via conformity with standards and procedures.

ANALYSE AND REVIEW	* Compare results against standards, targets, budgets.
	* Analyse issues arising, performance gaps, trends.
	* Assess overall performance of each function.

REPORT AND TAKE ACTION	* Presents results in appropriate format to internal audiences (staff, directorate, committee).
	* Communicate key results to tenants/consumers.
	* Respond to feedback, act to improve service, reward success, address weakness.

Figure 4.6   Key elements for improving housing performance

The Accounts Commission has promoted good practice but has also encouraged local authorities to develop review processes and approaches to performance management which match their local circumstances. Midwinter and Monaghan have commented on the difference between the Commissions proposing that:

> The Audit Commission for Local Authorities in England and Wales has specified a uniform evaluation model to be applied by auditors. Contrastingly, in Scotland, the Accounts Commission issued guidelines and an 'exemplified approach' which were to provide a framework within which auditors had, and indeed have, flexibility to derive their own detailed manuals of guidance for staff engaged in value for money. This seems a more appropriate way of operating than the previous method since recognition of local operating conditions is essential if value for money is to become meaningful and against this backdrop, flexibility and to some degree discretion seems fundamental.
> (Midwinter and Monaghan, 1993, p106)

Like the Audit Commission, the Accounts Commission's agenda in recent years has been dominated by preparation for and implementation of the Citizen's Charter and thus they have not issued an updated performance review guide since 1992. However, in anticipation of local authorities bearing the responsibility for implementing arrangements for securing economy, efficiency and efficiency, the Commission is currently developing a management arrangements guide. This is being compiled with support from councils and is currently being piloted in selected local authorities for planned implementation in the first operational year of the new unitary councils (Accounts Commission, 1995a). It is not yet available in the public domain but it is not anticipated that it will represent a significant deviation from the previous approach recommended by the Accounts Commission.

Alternative approaches to performance review

As previously indicated, much of the commentary surrounding value for money and performance review has centred on the definition and measurement of performance indicators (Beeton, 1988). As Pollitt (1989) has commented:

> There is now a substantial body of literature on the introduction of performance indicators to the major public services. Most commentators, however, have been concerned with the characteristics of particular indicators and with the pressures which led to their adoption in the first place.
> (Pollitt, 1989, p51)

Consequently, there are few developed approaches to performance review apart from those proposed by the Commissions. However, there are a couple of contributions which are worthy of consideration particularly for identifying any issues not exposed by either the Audit or Accounts Commissions which may need to be considered in undertaking research in the performance review area.

Henry Butt and Robert Palmer of Price Waterhouse produced *Value for money in the public sector: the decision-maker's guide* in 1985 which was intended as 'a comprehensive guide to all aspects of value for money in the public sector' (1985, jacket cover) and which Elcock et al. have described as 'an unusually comprehensive guide to value for money' (1989, p155). This sets out an approach to 'organising for value for money in local authorities' (1985, p23). The stages of this process are as shown below.

AGREE STRATEGIC BUDGET
↓
PRIORITY BASED BUDGET,
AGREE SERVICE LEVELS
↓
AGREE OPERATIONAL OBJECTIVES
AND TARGETS IN ANNUAL PLAN
↓
AGREE KEY PERFORMANCE
MEASURES AND STANDARDS
↓
AGREE ROLLING REVIEW PROGRAMME

Different parts of this process may be influenced by the Council, policy committee or management team.

This is supported by a 14 key point action plan for securing value for money as indicated in box 4.1. Whilst the action plan is arguably over ambitious for most local authorities, it again highlights the need for a link to be made with the budgetary process which they propose should be prioritised or zero based, and a distinction is drawn between the systematic, continuous ongoing review of performance with respect to both strategy and operations, and one-off, in depth reviews of service areas where there may be an indication that a problem exists.

Box 4.1:   Butt and Palmer's 14 key point action plan for securing value for money

1   Total commitment by senior elected representatives and officials. Right attitude to achieving value for money should permeate whole organisation.

2   Small, powerful but representative committee to direct and co-ordinate value for money projects.   Corporate approach to value for money should be adopted.

3   Clearly defined strategic and operational objectives and targets for all functions and activities.

4   Priority based or zero based budgeting approach whereby budget items are ranked for priority and the incremental effects of service level changes are calculated.

5   Key performance measures used for all major functions to evaluate and monitor productivity and effectiveness.

6   Performance measures linked to performance targets or standards for operational management so that productivity gains achieved during value for money reviews are maintained or improved upon.

7   A 'rolling' cost based review covering all areas of material spending and linked to the budgeting process. Particular attention to be paid to the cost of administration and supervision, energy and supplies. Management should be prepared to tackle 'soft' areas (e.g. education) as well as 'hard' areas (e.g. transport).

8   Regular comparisons with the costs and performance applying in the private sector for all services where it is appropriate to do so. Where better cost effectiveness can be obtained outside the organisation managers should be asked to justify keeping the service in-house.

Box 4.1: (continued)

9   Select for review only those areas with 'payback' potential. Areas of greatest materiality, or those which have known problems or those with a history of significant improvement in other organisations, should be considered first. 'Pilot' studies are useful to ensure that limited review resources are not wasted. Studies should cross departmental boundaries, for areas such as transport, to ascertain what scope exists for 'pooling.'

10   Investment made in people or equipment which will save money within a reasonable payback period (ideally 2/3 years) e.g. energy conservation officers and monitoring equipment, contract audit specialists, 'cook-chill' catering equipment.

11   Effective procedures to ensure that there is proper control over scarce resources e.g. for identifying surplus land, overstocking, unbanked cash, overmanning.

12   Consumer and 'client' surveys on a sample basis to test the quality of services e.g. exit questionnaires for mature students.

13   Budget process to encourage the controlled use of virement. Other incentives to achieving value for money such as performance bonuses should be considered.

14   Officials should be trained in management as well as technical matters.

(Butt and Palmer, 1985, p23)

However within their approach, there seems to be a heavy emphasis on savings and fiscal containment. The process also appears to be very mechanistic but the authors have indicated that:

> It cannot be stressed enough that value for money is not just a collection of techniques. It is above all an attitude of mind, a commitment to good practice on the part of politicians and officials. Having said that, value for money cannot be achieved by merely inspiring the necessary crusading spirit. Management's enthusiasm and drive has to be supported by the right organisational structure and also formalised budgeting, evaluation and monitoring systems.
> (Butt and Palmer, 1985, p22)

Commitment to the process is stressed not just from the top organisational tier but cascading throughout the local authority.

Robert Palmer, this time writing with Peter Jackson, has produced two further guides in the performance field. The first, *First Steps in Measuring Performance in the Public Sector: A Management Guide*, was published in 1989, and the second, *Developing Performance Monitoring in Public Sector Organisations: A Management Guide*, was produced in 1992. In the 1989 contribution, it was proposed that 'it is important that performance measures are matched to policy objectives, targets and activities for which specific managers have been allocated clear responsibility' (1989, p13). The specific steps involved in designing a performance measurement system as prescribed by Jackson and Palmer are:

1 DECIDE WHAT IS TO BE MEASURED

2 DECIDE WHAT MEASURES TO USE

3 ASCERTAIN SOURCES OF DATA

4 DESIGN SUPPORT SYSTEMS

They emphasize the need to select performance measures to match objectives finding comparators.

The Jackson and Palmer approach is very much focused on policy achievement although operational performance is not ignored and it is suggested that the performance of managers in relation to the areas for which they have responsibility be fed into a performance related pay scheme. The policy theme is continued in the 1992 publication where performance review is set within a complex strategic management process. Jackson and Palmer (1992) provide a summary and action plan for councils intending to introduce a performance management system. However, in the supporting commentary, the following advice is offered to those on the first rung of the performance review ladder:

> Strong senior management and political leadership; the unfreezing of prevailing attitudes of senior professional officers especially of the type that, 'the concept of objective setting and the measurement and assessment of outputs cannot be applied to my job', designing new information systems and the reorientation and training of staff are all necessary inputs to a performance review exercise.
> (Jackson and Palmer, 1992, p162)

They have observed that many public service organisations have found it useful to employ an external agency to act as a catalyst in getting the fundamental message of performance review across to the senior management team primarily because an external consultant can be more objective and is not part of the finely balanced political system of the internal organisation. They suggest that a typical way of approaching the problem of getting started and moving towards total organisational commitment is for the chief executive and senior managers and possibly members to participate in a number of residential weekend seminars led by the external consultant. During the course of the seminar a particular service is chosen to demonstrate how service objectives might be identified and how appropriate indicators relating to intermediate and final outputs and the 3Es etc. might be determined. Jackson and Palmer (1992) consider that this kind of exercise is useful in demonstrating to managers and politicians the potential value of performance review.

Having secured commitment to the concept of performance review the next step is deciding how to implement the review process. Jackson and Palmer (1992) argue that it is clear from an examination of the experiences of different public service organisations that no single ideal blueprint exists. In particular, they cite that local authorities all have different characteristics and different needs ranging from the closely knit small rural authority to the sprawling central city authority. The authors report that a choice faced by most organisations is whether or not to have a centralised performance review team whose purpose is to facilitate performance review throughout the organisation at a balanced and measured pace or to leave each service department to create its own performance review team. Jackson and Palmer report that many organisations have chosen to establish a centralised review team to get the system up and running but that the intention is then to dissolve the central team once the performance review process has matured, leaving a small central core to facilitate further developments with the major part of performance review work being undertaken by service departments. However, they also advocate that:

> Whichever structure is adopted a performance review group should not be left in isolation to determine its own fate. It must be keyed in to the regular reporting mechanisms of the organisation. Performance review groups themselves must pay particular attention to their own performance; what are their objectives, are they meeting them and are they giving value for money?
>
> (Jackson and Palmer, 1992, p163)

The authors indicate that the implementation process is likely to take several years and be an expensive exercise and that it is therefore necessary for those advocating its introduction to be ready to demonstrate that the benefits of a review outweigh the costs.

The 1992 guide contains a number of case studies but although performance measurement in a number of local authority service areas is considered, in particular, the library service, policing, education and social services, the approach which a local authority as a whole might pursue is not exemplified. Jackson and Palmer conclude their contribution by proposing that:

As in all spheres of management, there is no single best way of doing things. The procedures that you adopt for performance review will be contingent upon your local circumstances. Our framework represents a starting point for the design of your framework which will reflect your local conditions. Management systems evolve from experimentation, having an open mind and a willingness to learn and to cut and trim as circumstance change.

(Jackson and Palmer, 1992, p167)

Summary

This chapter has considered the recommended approaches to performance review which are in the public domain. No consensual impression of performance review emerged from examining these alternative processes but there were some common themes:

1   All of the approaches stressed that commitment to performance review was critical.

2   In varying degrees, the approaches acknowledged the need to differentiate between performance in relation to policies and operations. The Audit Commission whilst recognising the need to consider service effectiveness did not discuss this within the context of policies and advocated the use of proxy measures in this domain.

3   De-emphasising the local policy dimension accounts for the Audit Commission's bias towards comparing performance with external criteria where the other approaches stress measurement against internally determined targets and standards.

4   With the exception of the Audit Commission, performance review is perceived as an integral part of a wider management process and Jackson and Palmer particularly see it as being integrated into a complex strategic management framework.

5   The Accounts Commission and Butt and Palmer particularly stress the need to link performance review with the budgetary process.

6   The Audit Commission and Jackson and Palmer highlight the potential role to be played by a performance review team, both perceiving this to be catalytic.

However, there were also some issues only highlighted in one of the approaches:

1   Only the Audit Commission emphasised the significance of quality in the performance of services but recognised the measurement difficulties which this posed.

2   Jackson and Palmer see the results of performance review as feeding into performance related pay for managers.

3   The above authors also see a role for external consultants in getting the process off the ground and argue that the implementation process is likely to be long and expensive.

4   Only in Butt and Palmer's approach is a distinction drawn between systematic, continuous, on-going review and one-off, in-depth reviews normally initiated when some thing appears to be wrong in a particular service area.

None of the mechanisms seem based on the experiences of local authorities but are rather postulated as best practice without substantiation.

The purpose of considering these approaches was to identify some the key issues which need to be considered in undertaking a critique of performance review activity and to allow comparisons to be made between the systems identified as in operation in local authorities and the advocated approaches. These issues are explored in our research work which is reported in the two subsequent chapters.

5 Performance review: an overall picture

Introduction

Our research work on performance review systems had two overall objectives. These were:

1 To gain a general picture of performance review work in British local government. This would include viewing problems of developing and setting up systems, political control, linkages with other systems and potential future changes and developments.
2 To study a small number of systems in detail to gain a detailed insight into the development of different types of systems and problems associated with their operation.

The first objective can best be addressed using a written questionnaire. The details of this part of the study are covered in the current Chapter. The second study is best approached using a case study approach including in-depth interviews with officers and members. This will be covered in the following chapter.

Questionnaire survey

Since the purpose of the survey was to get as broad a picture as possible of performance review work in Great Britain, it was decided to contact all councils rather than adopt a sampling approach. It was decided to address questionnaires to chief executives which would particularly focus on managerial issues and separate ones to council leaders which would focus on more political matters.
In particular, the chief executive's questionnaire would focus on:

1 Problems of establishing a performance review system.
2 Problems of operating a performance review system.

3   Linkages with other systems (strategic planning and budgetary systems).
4   Corporate and developmental issues.
5   Potential future changes to the system.

Council leaders were asked about the political dimension including the roles of the majority and minority group.

Councils not operating performance review systems were asked questions about mechanisms that they adopt to review performance and whether they might adopt a performance review system in the future. Where a council had abandoned its performance review system it was of particular interest to explore its reasons for doing so.

The scale of performance review in Great Britain

Overall 262 questionnaires were returned from chief executives and 187 from council leaders. This represents a 55 per cent and 41 per cent response rate respectively. Such a response rate is sufficiently high to give a representative picture.

Details of responses from different types of authority are outlined below in Table 5.1.

Table 5.1
Participation in research

	Number of authorities	Chief executive participation response rate (%)	Council leader participation response rate (%)
London boroughs	33	72.7	57.6
Scottish regions	12	83.3	50.0
Scottish districts	53	64.2	41.2
Welsh counties	8	62.5	50.0
Welsh districts	37	37.8	24.3
County councils	39	69.2	51.3
Metropolitan districts	36	44.4	36.1
Non-metropolitan districts	296	52.4	39.5
TOTAL	**514**	**55.4**	**40.9**

In some authorities responses were received from both chief executives and leaders, whilst in others we received responses from either chief executive only or leader only.

If we amalgamate these responses we get the data shown in Table 5.2.

Table 5.2

The incidence of performance review in the UK*

	Number operating review procedures (1)	% of total authorities (2)	% of responding authorities (3)	Number not operating review procedures (4)	% of total authorities (5)	% of responding authorities (6)
London boroughs	21	63.6	87.5	3	9.1	12.5
Scottish regions	7	58.3	63.6	4	33.3	36.4
Scottish districts	18	34.0	46.2	21	39.6	53.8
Welsh counties	3	37.5	37.5	5	62.5	62.5
Welsh districts	5	13.5	29.4	12	32.4	70.6
County councils	25	64.1	86.2	4	10.3	13.8
Metropolitan districts	12	33.3	66.6	6	16.7	33.3
Non-metropolitan districts	94	31.7	56.3	73	24.7	43.7
TOTAL	**185**	**36.0**	**59.1**	**128**	**24.9**	**40.9**

Note * Includes authorities who did not complete the questionnaire but who communicated whether or not they operated a formalised review system.

89

This table indicates that 185 (36 per cent) of councils in this country operate performance review systems while 128 (25 per cent) do not. A further 201 (39 per cent) failed to respond.

It might be reasonable to assume that authorities not operating such systems might have a higher non response rate, although there is no definite evidence to support such an hypothesis. Even allowing for this, however, it seems highly likely that at least half of all authorities operate some kind of performance review mechanism.

In Table 5.2, column (2) gives the percentage of authorities operating performance review systems in relation to *all* authorities (whether or not they responded to the questionnaire) whereas column (3) gives the percentage of responding authorities. Columns (5) and (6) give the same measures for those authorities *not* operating performance review systems.

Results show that large authorities such as county councils, London boroughs and Metropolitan districts tends to have a high incidence of performance review systems in place (although the low response rate from Metropolitan districts leaves an element of doubt).

This is perhaps not surprising. Smaller authorities may find it difficult to commit the necessary resources and can argue that they can 'see' what their performance is and, therefore, benefits from a formal review system are less. Nevertheless, some small authorities such as Arun and Wyre have developed comprehensive performance review systems.

Origins of the systems

The evidence shows that the vast majority of the performance review systems were introduced since the late 1980s. A small number date from the mid 1980s and even fewer from the local government reforms of the mid seventies and the recommendation of the Bains committee (1972) with regard to performance review. This timing is in keeping with the increased prominence which performance review and value for money issues have known since the late 1980s as evidenced by the Audit Commission's (1986) publication 'Performance Review in Local Government - a handbook for auditors and local authorities'. The timing also accords with the fiscal stress experienced by councils, the compulsory competitive tendering legislation and enhanced politicisation of local government.

It might be anticipated that in many cases the current performance review system would be based on an earlier system. This proved, in fact, to be the situation in 41.5 per cent of cases where a previous review process had operated prior to the introduction of the existing system. Furthermore in 18.9 per cent of responses the current system is an enhanced or modified version of the previous system. The proportion of existing systems which are revisions of earlier processes is highest in the London boroughs (80.0 per cent) and lowest in county councils (23.1 per cent). Additional comments to this question revealed that existing systems tended to be replaced by completely new systems where a major change such as a fundamental restructuring had been undertaken. More limited changes tended to result in modifications to or enhancements of existing systems.

Setting up a performance review system

Setting up a performance review system involves some individual or group driving the concept forward. Such development may be beset with a range of difficulties and depends on support from officers and members. These issues will be investigated below.

(i) Initiating the system

This issue was covered in both chief executive and leaders' questionnaire. Chief executive responses to the question about who initiated the performance review system are given below.

Table 5.3
Who initiated the proposal to introduce
performance review? (Chief executives' responses)

Response category	Total	Percentage
Officer	65	42.4
Officer and member	34	22.1
Members	19	12.4
Chief executives	19	12.4
Chief executive and leader	4	2.6
Chief officer	3	2.0
Consultants	3	2.0
Chief executive and member	1	0.7
Leader	1	0.7
Previous chief executive	1	0.7
District auditor	1	0.7
Nil response	2	1.3
TOTAL	**153**	**100.0**

The above responses indicate that in 58 per cent of cases the initiative was principally officer led, in 13 per cent member led and in 26 per cent of cases the proposal came jointly from officers and members. Little difference between authority type was discernible except that in three non metropolitan districts the proposal to introduce performance review came from consultants and in one case from the district auditor.

91

Rather a different response was obtained from council leaders.

Table 5.4
Who initiated the proposal to introduce
performance review? (Leaders' responses)

Response category	Total	Percentage
Officers	31	21.2
Officers and members	53	36.3
Members	50	34.2
Chief executive	3	2.1
Chief executive and leader	3	2.1
Consultants	2	1.3
Policy committee	1	0.7
Chief executive and chair	1	0.7
Reorganisation	1	0.7
Nil response	1	0.7
TOTAL	**146**	**100.0**

It is, perhaps, not surprising that the above table tells a different story, suggesting a much enhanced level of member involvement. According to these responses, members took the lead in 34 per cent of cases with joint member/officers working in about 39 per cent of cases. Closer examination of the data indicated that the inconsistency could not be explained by the fact that not all councils had submitted responses from both Chief Executive and Leader. It is, however, perhaps not unusual for different groups to retrospectively view the same events in quite distinct ways.

(ii) Support from members and officers

Establishment of an effective performance review system requires support of members and officers. This issue was taken up in detail in the chief executive's questionnaire.

Obviously commitment from the chief executive himself is fundamental to the successful establishment of a performance review system. Of the 121 chief executives who had been in post when the performance review system was introduced, only five reported themselves to have been unsupportive (four in non metropolitan districts, one in a Scottish district). Thirty two respondents had not been in post at the time but all reported that they would have been supportive had they been in office.

This high proportion of committed chief executives is not surprising since, although the chief executive does not need to be actively involved in the development of the system, his/her endorsement is required to give the process impetus and to ensure as far as possible chief officers take performance review seriously.

Support from chief officers is not quite so emphatic. If we aggregate responses received on officer support for performance review we get the following (Table 5.5).

Table 5.5
Officer support for performance review

	Number	Percentage
Supportive	123	80.3
Mixed	22	14.4
Unsupportive	7	4.6
Too soon to say	1	0.7
TOTAL	**153**	**100.0**

Resistance from a few service directors is not unusual. They resent the additional burden it will place on their already overworked departments, regarding the system as either an 'add on' or a move by the centre to monitor departmental activities. A further question indicated similar levels of chief officer support once the system had been introduced.

Member support is clearly essential for effective implementation of any system. Even if it is possible to implement a system, without member commitment it will be ineffective and likely to be abandoned once real difficulties appear. In the case studies it was found that a number of authorities regarded performance review as primarily a management tool and the issue of member commitment was either underplayed or ignored. Since performance review should be intimately linked to the policy process and since members are, at least in principle, policy makers, such an approach may well turn out to be rather short sighted. Table 6 below gives chief executives' assessments of member support for performance review.

Table 5. 6
Member support for performance review

	Number	Percentage
Supportive	140	91.4
Mixed	9	5.9
Unsupportive	1	0.7
Indifferent	3	2.0
TOTAL	**153**	**100.0**

Following implementation of the system the percentage in support dropped a little.

Our research indicated that around 50 per cent of authorities had introduced specific measures to enhance co-operation. Box A contains a subset of the most pertinent, revealing and frequently recurring answers.

Box A : Measures introduced to enhance officer/member co-operation

Regular chief executive/leader meetings and extended use of informal member/officer groups.

Members are kept informed of targets and the review process and would be informed by the chief executive of any drastic departure from targets.

The system is being developed through the consent and support of officers and members. There has been joint awareness training and a newly established group of chief officers and members will be involved in its development.

Joint officer/member informal seminars on policy formulation and strategic direction but this is wider than service by service performance review.

Through the interface created by meetings of the Audit Panel.

Chief officers and members are working together on agreeing a corporate plan and a statement in relation to what this county council does.

An officer performance review group chaired by the chief executive's policy assistant feeds into the main performance review committee.

Full debate with members as appropriate at committees. Also an informal arena has been created for chief officers and all members to discuss policy and performance issues.

At the start, middle and end of the performance review, the corporate management team consult the two members designated to assist with the review.

Rolling programme of review and discussion sessions.

Service plan panel meetings - informal meetings to discuss individual services whereby members have an opportunity to review performance, discuss any issues and agree targets.

Small working groups have been established to focus on the area of performance review that members are principally interested in.

It can be seen that a wide range of measures are used from informal member/officer groups to rolling programmes of review and discussion sessions.

Another approach for achieving officer commitment is linking the system to performance appraisal and performance related pay. This is covered in a subsequent section related to linkages.

In spite of these measures, however, many chief executives admitted real difficulties in establishing performance review systems. Over half (52.9 per cent) admitted encountering such difficulties and 3.3 per cent responded that it was too soon to say.

Chief executives were asked to elaborate on the nature of such difficulties. A content analysis of such responses is shown in Table 5.7.

Table 5.7
Major problems encountered in setting up
performance review systems

	Number	Percentage
Behavioural	44	33.0
Technical	42	31.6
Resources	34	25.6
Political	11	8.3
Linkage	2	1.5
TOTAL	**133**	**100.0**

The specific behavioural difficulties reported have primarily been lack of support from members and officers and problems with the organizational culture. The major technical difficulty has been designing appropriate performance indicators. Training and information management have been the major resource issues.

A selection of typical responses is included in Box B.

Box B: Difficulties encountered in setting up the performance review system

Reluctance of some chief officers to introduce targeting; lack of interest of some members; culture not supportive of performance measurement; continual budget reductions; difficulty in defining sensitive performance indicators.

Attitudes of some managers; the overheads of monitoring certain indicators and the paperwork presented at committee.

It was a top-down process introduced by members and imposed corporately. The main problem was that of getting ownership of the process by managers at all levels of the organization particularly at first line management level.

Ambiguous accountabilities; lack of management information; centralised control; and lack of customer orientation.

Members' understanding of the concept; seen as method of 'sorting out' the officers; following initial period (to 1976) when the council had majority rule, the council became hung and performance review was used as a tool for inter party debate and differences.

Whilst not a *major* problem, both officers and members were concerned about the setting of explicit targets because of the risk of failing to meet them and this being treated negatively by opposition groups on the council or by the public.

Finding worthwhile PIs; keeping scrutiny at the right level (e.g. avoiding detailed review of operational matters and focusing on overall performance of policies).

Some reluctance to change traditional ways of thinking, that is to make the cultural change required in order to focus more on outputs and outcomes rather than simply inputs.

All change is feared, particularly when it exposes individual performance. The education process has a distance to go still.

Low level of awareness of full potential of performance review among the members and some officers, caused limited degree of support. This was compounded by some services being dealt with at too operational a level for members' interests. Process is still being developed to address these and in particular to develop the role of members.

Sustaining momentum.

Senior staff could not see the advantages; staff felt threatened; and performance indicators have been difficult to agree.

It is clear that setting up a performance review system is not necessarily straightforward and is influenced by a range of factors. Clearly, the greater the ownership and commitment shown by officers and members, the less likely major problems will be encountered during the set up process.

Political control and performance review

We wished to investigate whether setting up a performance review system was likely to be influenced by the political party in charge of the council. Political control of respondent councils who had such systems is given in Table 5.8.

Table 5.8
Which party has overall political control
in your council? (Leader's responses)

Party	Number of councils	Percentage
Labour	58	39.7
Conservative	41	28.1
Liberal democrat	12	8.2
Other	13	8.9
None	22	15.1
TOTAL	**146**	**100.0**

Category 'other' contains authorities controlled by a minor party such as the Scottish National Party or a coalition. 'None' indicates no arrangements for control or an independent council. These figures were consistent with the pattern of political control at the time the study was carried out. We therefore concluded that the existence or otherwise of a performance review system was not linked to party political control.

Council leaders were asked about the role that the majority group play in the performance review process. A range of the most revealing answers is given in Box C.

Box C: What role does the majority group play in the performance review process?

Overall supervision.

The executive of the majority group meets on a fortnightly basis with senior officers to monitor/review key performance indicators. The majority group is involved in the selection of indicators annually.

Chair of policy oversees the performance review process; chair and vice chairs of service committees present relevant information on their departments to the chair of policy.

The performance review committee regularly receives reports on selected service areas regarding performance across the borough. Standing neighbourhood committees (or their sub committees) receive reports as requested, comparing performance in that neighbourhood with results achieved elsewhere so that neighbourhoods can learn from each other.

Decide areas for review.

Information relating to performance against targets is fed into annual departmental service development plans and used as part of the decision making process to determine the allocation of funding in committee.

The majority group sets objectives and agrees targets and performance standards for services in consultation with the chief executive and his management team.

Party groups do not play any role in the process as it is at panel, sub-committee and main committee level that members get involved in setting and monitoring performance, for example through the annual key tasks system.

The performance review process is now embodied into the work of committees of the city council, in particular the management services committee which plays a leading role. The majority group, through holding the chairmanship of various committees, therefore has an important role in ensuring that the process succeeds.

They have the major input together with chief officers to the policy planning process and agreeing the principal corporate and departmental objectives. Progress is regularly reported to all members. The majority group controls priorities.

The majority group sets direction, identifies objectives and decides on action resulting from review.

Identification of in-depth projects for review; sets down broad overall political objectives on which policy and performance review system is based.

Close scrutiny of reported performance; directs and takes corrective action necessary.

Content analysis revealed that responses could be divided into one of four categories.

Active As indicated by the response 'the majority group sets direction, identifies objectives and decides on action resulting from review' or, for example, by setting the performance agenda for the authority and relevant committees and identifying areas for review; and setting standards and/or defining indicators of performance.

Passive For example, as indicated by the response 'through the committee process' or by the councillor's role being confined to receiving regular performance information but with no indication given that much was done with the information or by 'supervising' the process.

Delegation Predominately to group officers as in the response 'the chair of policy oversees the performance review process; chair and vice chairs of service committees present relevant information on their departments to the chair of policy'.

Minimal Where the council leader considered that the majority group played no role in the review system.

Not all responses fitted neatly into one of these categories. Around 30 per cent indicated an active involvement, with a further 16 per cent reporting that participation in performance review was confined to key members of the majority party, particularly committee chairs (delegation category). Only 4 per cent of groups are not involved at all. The rest take a passive role as discussed above.

As might be expected, minority groups played a much less active role in the performance review process. Only about 3 per cent of minority groups played an active role with the rest either having no role (about 20 per cent) or a passive one (about 77 per cent).

Performance review systems should indicate the extent to which an authority has delivered its key objectives. Clearly, this should provide opportunities for both administration and opposition to use the system for party political purposes. Indeed, the leader of one council who had reservations about performance review described the process as the 'administration baring its soul'. Thus, council leaders were asked whether the performance review system was used for party political purposes by the majority and minority groups. Results are given in Table 5.9.

Table 5.9
Is the performance review system used
for party political purposes?

	Majority group		Minority group	
	No	%	No	%
Yes	44	30.2	21	14.4
No	69	47.3	86	58.9
Not systematically	12	8.2	13	8.9
Too early to say	5	3.4	8	5.5
Not applicable	6	4.1	5	3.4
Nil response	10	6.8	13	8.9
TOTAL	**146**	**100.0**	**146**	**100.0**

Thus, it seems relatively few minority group leaders use the performance review process for political ends. Nevertheless, our interviews with opposition leaders suggested considerable interest in and support for the concept of a performance review system.

A further aspect of the political dimension we need to consider is whether political objectives are incorporated in the performance process. Results from council leaders are shown below (Table 5.10).

Table 5.10
Are political objectives incorporated into
the performance review process?

	Number	Percentage
Yes	91	62.3
No	39	26.7
Not systematically	8	5.4
Too early to say	3	2.1
Not applicable	3	2.1
Nil response	2	1.4
TOTAL	**146**	**100.0**

At first glance, it may seen surprising that over a quarter of council leaders reported that performance review systems do not accommodate the objectives of the ruling group. Closer scrutiny, however, reveals that in 26 of the 39 negative responses given, the council leader represented either a hung council or one in which no overall political control was exercised.

Those leaders who indicated that the objectives of their administration was integrated into the performance review process were asked to indicate how this had been achieved. This is shown in Box D overleaf. It can be seen that some authorities suggest working to establish their key tasks or targets whilst others are more comprehensive and link to the strategic or service planning system.

Box D: How are the political objectives of your administration incorporated into the performance review system?

Through (i) committee agreement of targets for services; and (ii) each committee's three year plan details strategic developments which translate into targets for services.

Political objectives form the basis of the system of targets.

The majority party has established ten tasks. The system is designed to provide information on the extent to which these are being achieved.

The review of performance relates to the objectives of the county council as detailed in the council council's policy budget. The policy budget contains the overall strategy of the county council, its service bloc strategies, policy objectives and medium term action programme and annual plans. Performance review enables an assessment of the progress of the medium term action programme and of the council's overall strategy.

Only in the sense that key objectives for the year are identified and these are related to the high priority tasks which committees (upon which the conservative group form the majority) identify as requiring particular attention.

The performance targets are geared to the policy objectives of the controlling group.

In ensuring that the underlying ethos is maintained throughout the review of the service.

Quality audit mentality.

We ensure that budget allocations and monitoring is focused on our priorities.

Through strategy and service plans.

Within the council's corporate strategy, each committee's aims and objectives, through a series of targeted key tasks, and in the establishment of working groups.

Organisational issues

There are a number of organisational issues related to how performance review fits into the political and managerial structure of the council to be addressed. One such issue is to where (if at all) performance review fits into the council's committee structure (table 5.11 Chief Executives' response).

Table 5.11
Which committee is responsible for performance review?

	Number	Percentage
All committees	34	22.2
Policy and resources	23	15.0
Performance review	23	15.0
All service committees	12	7.9
Policy	11	7.2
Policy & resources and service committees	6	3.9
None specifically	4	2.6
Performance review and service committees	3	2.0
Quality service sub-committee	2	1.3
Policy and review	2	1.3
A finance sub committee	2	1.3
Policy, resources and performance review	2	1.3
Other	26	17.0
Nil response	3	2.0
TOTAL	**153**	**100.0**

A common response was that performance review was the responsibility of all committees or at least of all service committees. This has the advantage that committees who are responsible for services are also responsible for monitoring performance. Other councils have separate performance review committees or give the responsibility to policy and resources. This, however, may break the link between responsibility for a service and its monitoring process.

There is also a question about how performance review fits into the council's management structure. A wide range of answers was given by the Chief Executives but they were grouped together (Table 5.12).

Table 5.12
How does the PR system fit into corporate management structure?

		Number	Percentage
1	Through management team/board	54	35.3
2	Through chief executive	19	12.4
3	Through chief officers	15	9.8
4	Through all managers	10	6.5
5	PR system fully integrated	9	5.9
6	Through policy unit	7	4.6
7	Other	23	15.0
8	Nil response	16	10.5
	TOTAL	**153**	**100.0**

In the majority of cases the council's management team operates as the interface between the performance review system and the corporate management structure. Overall, in 88 (57.5 per cent) of local authorities the performance review system fits into the corporate management structure. Such senior involvement suggests that performance review is given a high priority in a significant number of councils.

The other outstanding managerial question is the designation of staff with responsibility for performance review and staff who were responsible for carrying out the work. This is shown in Table 5.13 below.

Table 5.13
The designated officer with performance review responsibility

	Number	Percentage
Chief executive	29	19.0
Chief officers	19	12.4
Corporate staff	16	10.5
Assistant chief executive	15	9.8
Policy staff	11	7.2
Performance review staff	8	5.2
Service managers	6	3.9
Management services staff	6	3.9
No specific responsibility assigned	6	3.9
All senior managers	4	2.6
All staff	3	2.0
Other	27	17.6
Nil response	3	2.0
TOTAL	**153**	**100.0**

Twenty nine (19.0 per cent) of chief executives reported that they were the officer within the authority with responsibilities for performance review. Nineteen (12.4 per cent) reported that all chief officers had such responsibilities and in a further 15 (9.8 per cent) of cases the assistant chief executive was responsible. Quite a few answers were given that did not fit into any standard format including management development unit, head of consultancy service and second tier managers.

The systems and their linkages

We first of all wish to explore certain aspects of the system including the performance measures and indicators used together with its linkages to other systems. As we have seen in earlier chapters, monitoring the extent to which policy objectives and targets are achieved is of crucial importance. Many of the responses from chief executives suggest that the measures/indicators used are extremely operational if not management statistics. Some authorities seem content simply to adopt Audit Commission indicators for this purpose. Box E below illustrates some of the most common responses.

Box E: How were performance measures set for the performance review system?

Customer service driven.

Defined by heads of service in business plans.

Consideration of key service areas by management team.

Consultative mechanism starting with the Audit Commission statistics. These are still being refined.

These were developed by managers in liaison with the policy unit.

Via the 'quality assurance' panel of members.

Initially they were set by the management services unit staff and modified by departmental managers. They were based on Audit Commission information and research information elsewhere.

Reference to the approach adopted in other authorities but with emphasis on quality based performance indicators.

Based on a formula provided by consultants.

Largely by reference to Audit Commission suggestions. This has evolved since performance review has been embarked upon and the business planning process is helping to focus minds.

Based upon measured customer/client expectations. Agreed targets set between staff and directors.

Mainly the achievement of key tasks within timetables. Certain measures relate to norms.

Chief executives were asked about who was responsible for setting the measures/indicators. This is illustrated below in Table 5.14.

Table 5.14
Who set the measures/indicators?

	Total	Percentage
Officers	71	46.4
Jointly set	36	23.5
Committees	20	13.0
Members	7	4.6
Other	7	4.6
Ongoing	3	2.0
Not set/agreed	1	0.7
Nil response or N/A	9	5.2
TOTAL	**153**	**100.0**

This confirms that members' input is much more limited. It might be argued that members' main function is to articulate policy objectives and that the task of developing appropriate indicators is a more technical matter that can reasonably be left to officers.

In our discussion of the performance review literature we saw how different indicators relate to economy, efficiency and effectiveness and the importance of developing appropriate measures of effectiveness. Chief executives were asked to describe how their indicators/measures distinguish between economy, efficiency and effectiveness. Some of the responses are shown in Box F.

Box F: Details of how performance measures distinguish between economy, efficiency and effectiveness

Measures are still straightforward financial ratios but information is provided, for example, on success rate in planning appeals, HSE notices etc.

Indicators are presented/identified using the following headings: input/budget (economy); demand, productivity and output (efficiency); and outcome/quality and customer service standards (effectiveness).

Economy - focus on costs e.g. inputs; *efficiency* - doing things right e.g. on time, turn around within target, general focus on outputs; *effectiveness* - doing the right thing e.g. customer satisfaction surveys, general focus on outcomes.

We have been trying to concentrate on output indicators; Value for Money is addressed by individual policy reviews on a five year cycle; the Audit Commission profiles are used as a first stage comparator.

Unit cost information and some information on effectiveness are included in PI reports.

Indicators are identified in relation to: cost of the service; amount of service available; amount of service used; quality and efficiency of the service; and value for money.

Implicitly if not explicitly. Whenever targets are set, they must if possible be quantifiable in some way - otherwise they cannot be measured.

Measures are set to develop and direct services by examining unit costs, inputs and outputs and using basic zero based budgeting.

Performance measures are linked to the strategic and operational objectives of the services concerned. Strategic objectives are concerned with effectiveness; operational objectives with economy and efficiency.

Utilise Audit Commission definitions.

The responses lacked any clear or consistent theme and this is clearly an area which causes managers real difficulties. Then the question arose as to whether authorities had perhaps used quality indicators as a surrogate for effectiveness. Almost 60 per cent of chief executives responded that such measures were indeed in use while in 5 per cent of cases they were under development. They were also asked to give examples of quality measures in use. This is given in Box G.

> *Box G: Examples of measures of quality utilised in performance review systems*
>
> Standards of housing repairs and maintenance; standards of refuse collection and street cleaning; and standards in education, particularly schools and exam results.
>
> Service standards; market research and the Citizen's Charter.
>
> Quality assurance standards.
>
> The objective of the system is all about quality. We are defining in advance what our customers need and expect, doing it and then asking them to review our performance.
>
> Annual user satisfaction surveys in urban improvement areas (planning).
>
> Audit Commission's quality exchange exercise.
>
> Examination results and pupils staying on rates; satisfaction surveys; successful prosecution rates on trading standards; ratio of planning appeals lost to total appeals; class days lost due to closure of buildings from failure of fabric or service. The above are just a selection of performance indicators which are more clearly measures (or indicators) of quality. The continuing challenge is to produce more indicators which measure quality of output/ outcome rather than quality and quantity of inputs.
>
> 'Quality' is understood as the aggregation of efficiency, effectiveness and economy which will ultimately be measured by separate indicators for each service.
>
> Customers assess the quality of service via questionnaires.
>
> Quality assurance and BSI accreditation being sought.

The majority of responses stress the importance of consumer's assessment of the service in any measure of quality.

We have now covered certain aspects of the performance review system but clearly for real effectiveness to be achieved we must ensure that appropriate links with the policy/strategic planning process and the budgeting process exist.

Responses to the question whether performance review is linked to the policy planning process is given below for both chief executives and members (Table 5.15).

Table 5.15

Is performance review linked to the policy planning process?

	Chief executive		Leader	
	No	%	No	%
Yes	114	74.5	99	67.8
No	24	15.7	28	19.2
Partially	-	-	9	6.2
Ongoing	11	7.2	9	6.2
Nil response	4	2.6	1	0.6
TOTAL	**153**	**100.0**	**146**	**100.0**

Considering the chief executive and leaders do not all originate from the same authorities, there is considerable measure of agreement that appropriate linkages between such systems are in place in most authorities. This then raises the question as to the nature of such links. Box H covers this issue.

Box H: How is the performance review system linked to the policy/strategic planning process?

Through committee agreement of targets for services and each committee's Three Year Plan details strategic developments which translate into targets for services.

Key tasks and review are part of the strategic plan for this authority.

Our system is a three stage cyclical process whereby review feeds into policy formulation which feeds into policy budgets which feeds back into review.

By virtue of monitoring and intuition by the corporate management team.

The planning process outlines the direction in which the county council is going and all Key Result Areas and Performance Standards need to be linked to this.

The policy planning/strategic planning process forms the basis of the performance review system.

Three year committee Service Plans are produced annually, containing targets and indicators where possible. Quarterly performance indicator reports are produced for each Committee - these refer inter alia to the plan targets.

Key priorities are sub-divided into objectives/targets for development which forms the basis of a measurable performance review system.

Each service will have a working group which will be comprised of members and officers. The group will look at service provision and then feed these ideas into the corporate planning process.

Through Service Plans.

Performance Review Sub-Committee looks at policy review. Policies/policy objectives are identified and effectiveness reviewed. Policy objectives will be fed into the strategic/business planning process which will be subject to performance review.

Provides information for Forward Planning Cycle.

Each department examines strategic objectives, from their business plans through to their own performance indicators.

Many authorities approach this using service/business plans or other documents. Some of the processes appear quite dynamic with findings emerging from the performance review system feeding into policy formulation and determining what needs to be the subject of scrutiny in future years. Some approaches such as the use of key tasks and monitoring and induction by the management team are much more ad hoc.

The responses do give rise to the question of what happens in councils in which performance review and policy planning are not linked. Such a process would appear to undermine the entire concept of performance review. It could be the case, however, that in some of these authorities performance review is confined to one-off efficiency studies.

Both sets of respondents were asked about linkages with the budgetary process. Responses to this question are given in Table 5.16.

Table 5.16
Is performance review linked to the budgetary process?

	Chief executive		Leader	
	No	%	No	%
Yes	94	61.4	98	67.1
No	47	30.7	31	21.2
Partially	-	-	6	4.1
Ongoing	9	5.9	8	5.5
Nil response	3	2.0	3	2.1
TOTAL	**153**	**100.0**	**146**	**100.0**

There are some interesting differences between chief executive and leader responses here, with a significantly higher proportion of chief executives believing that no linkage exists.

The authors' personal experience suggests proper linkage with the budgetary system is much more difficult to attain and this is borne out by much of the case study evidence. A sample of the responses to this question are given in Box I.

Box 1: How is the performance review process linked to the budgetary process?

The policy budget process will increasingly encourage past performance to be taken into account in resource allocation decisions.

Service plans are expected to demonstrate how proposals will progress the Council's strategic objectives which are then taken into account in budget allocations. The process is still fairly embryonic and requires considerable refinement.

The performance review system is linked to the budgetary process but not driven by it. There is a vast amount of work to be done before getting to the stage where policy decisions determine *all* spending priorities.

We are aiming to make the budget process more service and policy objective led but this will take time - it is like trying to change the direction of an ocean liner.

A review of performance takes place each autumn prior to the budget setting process and the results are fed into the process.

Intention is that performance indicators will be included in the budget book showing change over time.

Policy/strategic planning cannot be separated from budgetary planning.

Service plans are the first stage of the budget cycle each year.

Budgets (capital and revenue) are determined within a corporate cost-benefit framework based on overall objectives. The performance standards for each service reflect what is achievable within the level of resources allocated to a service via this process.

The whole budget/corporate planning/review systems are interlinked, although major reviews of performance are often undertaken for political reasons also.

Used to find options for change to meet capping level.

It will be noted that in many cases linkage was being developed but that progress was only gradual. The remark 'like trying to change the direction of an ocean liner' will strike a chord with many who are experienced in the area. Slow progress in this area might be anticipated given the huge volume of financial changes taking place in local government in the recent past and the long tradition of incremental budgeting that has characterised British local government.

If policy and budgeting processes are to be linked and we are to move from budget led decisions to policy led decisions, performance review will have an important role to play. One respondent indicated that performance review was used to find options for change to meet the capping level. Effectively, this is using the performance review process to finance the next round of cuts - likely to create a very negative image for performance review.

One criticism sometimes levelled at performance review systems is that sometimes they result in a narrowing of perspective and tasks that are not associated with the performance review system may be effectively ignored. To quote Romney et al, (1979):

> Eyes fixed only on the accomplishment of a measured set of institutional goals may become obstinate to change, to options, to courses of action. Such tunnel vision often develops a myopic vision of institutional purpose and activity. To carry the analogy a step further an associated consequence is the loss of peripheral vision or ability to sense and grasp opportunities. (Romney et al, 1979, p89)

Chief executives were asked what provision is made for monitoring tasks not specifically covered in the performance review system. A selection of the most significant responses is given in Box J.

Box J: What provision is made for monitoring and appraising tasks not incorporated into the performance review system?

Via chief officers and other appraisal processes - the performance review systems operates primarily at the strategic level of whole services.

By use of staff appraisals and departmental working plans.

Additional reviews.

Quarterly reports will include any unforeseen developments.

The county council departments are continually reviewing and revising their services in the light of changes in needs, legislation and to meet targets. Direct Service Organisations have their own statutory targets to meet and review their progress towards meeting these. The county treasurer continuously monitors the financial performance of departments and the county.

Performance appraisal, general departmental monitoring and supervisory procedures.

Performance measurement and monitoring is only part of performance review. A small group of senior members and officers consider and stimulate the review of any activity. Internal audit carries out wide ranging reviews as do individual chief officers.

Performance appraisal.

Appraisal covers both completion of targets and overall job performance.

The relevant committees can request specific reports covering areas of concern with the agreement of the policy committee.

Basic management responsibility.

Exception reporting to committee and performance appraisal.

Different services have their own ad hoc/informal measures for tasks which, whilst important to a section and its work programme would not be sufficiently high profile to be formally included in the corporate review system.

Many of these responses highlight that performance review and appraisal, departmental monitoring and ad hoc reviews ensure a broader perspective. Staff appraisals will generally look at across the board job performance rather than focusing in specific areas.

Corporate and development issues

The existence or otherwise of a performance review system is likely to influence the corporate values and culture of an organisation. We have discussed in the first Chapter about changing culture of local government. Our survey results suggest that around three-quarters of all chief executives felt that such an association did exist. Those respondents indicating that a change in corporate value/culture were asked to elaborate on the nature of the change. A subset of the most revealing responses is given in Box K.

Box K: Changes in corporate values/culture associated with the operation of the performance review system

We are now more customer orientated.

The introduction of performance review was consciously and explicitly associated with the efforts to change the culture of the organisation towards performance/customer orientation.

It has directly led to a revaluation of policies and objectives. This has in turn led to better definition of corporate values, management standards and disciplines, service standards, client/customer orientation and service guarantees.

More customer orientated; the introduction of quality measures; responsiveness to the recession; and the enabling culture.

Accountable/developed management : a clearer client/provider relationship; and more customer orientation in services.

Commitment to quality has been enhanced and there is an increased awareness of the 'customer'.

The introduction of performance review is a component of a package of measures designed to facilitate cultural change in the authority. These include enhancing the strategic and policy making role of members, improved member technical support, development of the county strategy, officer/member working groups, customer orientation and improved local accountability.

Focus on client needs.

Council has evolved clear customer care policies such as 'quality' culture - listening to customers, more questioning/awareness of what services are about. The introduction of a performance review system involves and requires major changes in values/culture, to one of putting the customer first.

Now greater awareness within the organisation of strategic aims of the council and how individual services contribute to these.

The process has caused cultural priorities and values to emerge as well as performance review goals, that is the way in which the goals are to be achieved has been put into context.

Change from finance led to policy led.

An acceptance that customers' attitudes and opinions have to be examined to specify services and service levels. Recognition of a general need to develop a more commercial management approach.

The system itself has been a means of changing culture by the establishment of targets and tasks which mirror a more modern culture.

A range of different changes in corporate values and culture is in evidence. A significant number of answers stress that operating a review system has introduced a new customer focus within the local authority with greater attention to what customers perceive their needs to be, leading to more customer oriented service provision. In other cases the establishment of the system has been the catalyst for delineating the council's aims and objectives and getting agreement between officers and members about what the organisation is trying to achieve.

This very much suggests that a corporate perspective is being developed and this issue was put to chief executives (Table 5.17).

Table 5.17
Do you feel that the system has contributed significantly towards achieving a corporate management perspective?

	No	Percentage
Yes	100	65.3
No	28	18.3
Too early	18	11.8
Nil response	8	4.6
TOTAL	**153**	**100.0**

Less than 20 per cent felt that the system had not contributed towards developing a corporate management perspective (of course such a perspective may still exist although performance review has not contributed towards achieving it).

Further, chief executives were asked whether the system had contributed to the achievement of corporate goals. Results are shown below (Table 5.18).

Table 5.18
Do you feel that the system has contributed towards achieving corporate goals?

	No	Percentage
Yes	92	60.1
No	30	19.6
Partially	7	4.6
Too early	17	11.1
Nil response	7	4.6
TOTAL	**153**	**100.0**

Slightly fewer chief executives indicated that the review system had not contributed towards achieving corporate goals; the main authority groupings in this category being Welsh authorities.

There are a number of development issues worthy of consideration. One such issue is to what extent the operation of such a system gives rise to additional training needs. Responses were as follows.

Table 5.19
Has the performance review system identified any training needs in relation to operating the system?

	No	Percentage
Yes	97	63.4
No	38	24.8
Too early	11	7.2
Nil response	7	4.6
TOTAL	**153**	**100.0**

The significant majority answering yes to this question indicates the need for authorities planning to introduce such systems to take potential development needs on board.

A further developmental issue is investigation of major changes that have been made to the system since its introduction. Around a quarter of all authorities had made such changes. Some of the most common responses are contained in Box L.

Box L: Major changes made to performance review system since its introduction

The incorporation of the Audit Commission's requirements for statutory indicators; the requirement for customer service standards linked with the Citizen's Charter.

It is currently under review to make it more strategic and less operationally focused.

Further coverage of services; more definitions to aid data comparability; spotlights on areas of special interest to management board; neighbourhood performance review sub-committee where the general public can take a greater interest.

Since 1990, annual reports contain performance indicators and key objectives are linked to targets and measures.

Emphasis shift to total quality management.

Extended to all committees.

Performance measures have been adopted to take account of the Audit Commission's *quality exchange* initiatives.

All members of the county council are invited to suggest new key tasks; and responsibility for monitoring key tasks is now being differentiated between main committees and sub committees.

Linking the performance review process more clearly with the policy planning process through including provision for service prioritisation, addressing strategic priorities. Move to make performance indicators more clearly related to service provision.

Performance indicators substantially updated.

Concentrated on fewer but better measures.

When first introduced, there was no standard authority wide process, which led to varying practices between committees and departments. A standard practice manual was then introduced, supported by officer training and a seminar with members. The process is currently under review after around 18 months in operation.

The introduction of trading accounts.

Originally the system applied to a small number of services, for whom it was easier to apply quantitative measures. The aim now is to have more qualitative measures and cover all services and council activities, internal and external.

A wide range of changes is in evidence, some extending the role and coverage of the review system but others indicating a rationalisation of its operations, for example, by focusing on fewer but more appropriate performance measures or by refocusing the review system to concentrate on more strategic issues. A number of chief executives also indicated that they had accommodated the Audit Commission's indicators. Surprisingly there seems little relationship between difficulties reported by chief executives in establishing the review system and changes that have been made in the review process.

Evaluation and future developments

Both chief executives and council leaders were asked to evaluate the success of the system. The results are as follows.

Table 5.20
Chief executive and council leader assessment
of performance review

	Chief executive		Leader	
	Number	%	Number	%
Successful	94	61.5	96	65.7
Not successful	8	5.2	13	8.9
Partially	5	3.3	7	4.8
Too early to say	38	24.8	28	19.2
Nil response	8	5.2	2	1.3
TOTAL	**153**	**100.0**	**146**	**100.0**

It is notable that few chief executives or council leaders believed that the performance review system has been unsuccessful, although a substantial number felt that it was too early to pass judgement. Many of the 'unsuccessful' responses came from 'smaller' types of authority. Figures from council leaders are very similar to those from chief executives. In cases where an unsuccessful or partially successful system was reported, various kinds of operational problems are generally associated with the lack of success. In 89 authorities, responses were supplied by both council leaders and chief executives. In these 80 produced the same response, all but two indicating success.

Both chief executives and leaders were asked what future developments they envisaged seeing in the system. Content analysis of the answers revealed the following results.

119

Table 5.21
Future developments
(some respondents supplied multiple responses)

Development	Chief officers		Leaders	
	No.	%	No.	%
Linkage	75	46.0	47	31.1
Behaviour/involvement	53	31.5	22	14.6
Technical	24	14.7	66	43.7
Planning processes	6	3.7	5	3.3
Resources	5	3.1	6	4.0
Committee	-	-	5	3.3
TOTAL	**163**	**100.0**	**151**	**100.0**

An interesting result is the divergence between chief officers and leaders. Chief officers are much more aware of the need to link performance review with other systems and technical improvements are given a relatively low priority. With council leaders, although linkages still have a high priority, technical improvements are ranked much more highly. This may indicate that leaders, perhaps misguidedly, are looking for a 'technical fix' to solve their problems.

Some typical responses from chief executives are shown in Box M and from leaders in Box N.

Box M: What do you see as the most significant future development resulting from operation of the performance review system? (chief executives)

The development of an integrated strategic planning and review process across the council; and the development of a performance culture.

Improved performance arising from the clarification of the roles of all employees, with due regard to the council's corporate and developmental objectives.

Greater clarity of purpose and direction; improved corporate working; and the provision of benchmarks to measure progress in key areas.

Our system will be related to Accounts Commission proposals on an external level. Internally, for each specified activity we intend to develop quality targets to enable us to assess our performance.

The identification of a managerial and political consensus around a common purpose.

Performance review is a key component in a strategic change package which should facilitate the acceptance and enthusiastic implementation of performance management as a process *owned* by departments, and leading to greater sense of purpose, direction and accountability.

Client committees focusing on policies, achievement, relevance of activity undertaken rather than the efficiency of delivery.

Closer links with the budgetary process and developments arising from the implementation of proposals in the Citizen's Charter.

Ability to plan service delivery in the light of agreed priorities, and able to measure the effect of those priorities.

Greater member awareness as to strategic levels and quality and to the best use of resources.

The most significant development from our system must be the ability to establish accurately whether departments are providing the service which the members require them to.

Ability to cope with uncertain financial and political climate.

Better allocation of resources, clearer acknowledgement of priorities; clearer individually defined accountabilities.

Integration of systems, better 'control' over the very diverse range of local government services, enables better delegation without abdication of responsibility, and framework for setting targets, linked to resources and choices of priorities.

Greater emphasis on outputs rather than inputs.

Box M: Cont'd

Greater member concentration on core service standards rather than operational decisions and new developments at the margin.

The ability to judge where policy and performance is effective and efficient and to be able to identify weak areas. To have the information to decide what action should be taken. To improve priority setting. Improvement to policy implementation. Managers will have the information to control the work of their service so that it meets objectives.

Alignment of council activities with members' desires and consumer needs/demands.

Box N: What do you see as the most significant future development resulting from operation of the performance review system? (Council Leaders)

Extension of targeting to all major services; and the development of measures of consumer satisfaction within service targets.

Refining and fine tuning; linking it much more to sound external data - for example, the changing profile of the borough's population.

The incorporation of our recently launched Citizen's Charter into every department's key tasks.

Proper measurement of all functions and a system produced which will create improvements in these measurements.

I would like to link it to the political objectives in the manifesto and use it for strategic and financial planning.

The authority's objectives will be supported by output/outcome driven performance indicators.

I would like to see an outside moderator from another authority to sit in with the panels.

Clearly the Citizen's Charter performance indicators will be leading change in performance review in the next few years.

Consultation with customers.

Further development of corporate management; to date the system has concentrated on short term planning and objectives - the development of longer term policy planning and objectives must be a priority together with the development of more meaningful measures of performance.

Given the present state of local government, this performance review process will increasingly be called upon to indicate priorities.

We want it to be closely linked with our customer care programme so that we can monitor our services and take on board customer comments and so continually review and compromise.

What we need is performance review of our performance review system - and we are now in a position where a few senior members are at long last beginning to see the importance of performance review.

A comprehensive process incorporating: policy/planning and policy review; budgetary process; performance review within corporate strategic/business planning process; and the incorporation of survey and other qualitative information.

More measures of customer perception/satisfaction.

System which did not simply measure internal statistics - for example, outturn against budget - but also made measures in a league table type of monitoring against other authorities for a standard performance area. I would like the audit service to recommend best standard practice for most areas of service provision and organise their own computers to produce league tables of actual performance attained.

Getting the role of members clarified as at present members are involved in detail about service plan monitoring that we see as a management role; building members' performance into the system.

Cascading down through the organisation and greater understanding by members.

Councils not operating performance review systems

General

It is of major interest to investigate those authorities not running performance review systems. Issues of interest include whether such a system has operated in the past and been discontinued.

We saw from Table 5.2 that just over 40 per cent of respondents did not operate performance review procedures. These chief executives were asked if any mechanism for reviewing performance existed. Almost 50 per cent claimed that such mechanisms did exist. Those claiming such a mechanism were asked to elaborate. A selection of the most significant mechanisms is given in Box O.

Box O: Mechanisms used to review performance

Through committee agreement of targets for services and each committee's three year plan details strategic developments which translate into targets for services.

Key tasks and review are part of the strategic plan for this authority.

Our system is a three stage cyclical process whereby review feeds into policy formulation which feeds into policy budgets which feeds back into review.

By virtue of monitoring and intuition by the corporate management team.

The planning process outlines the direction in which the county council is going and all key result areas and performance standards need to be linked to this.

The policy planning/strategic planning process forms the basis of the performance review system.

Three year committee service plans are produced annually, containing targets and indicators where possible. Quarterly performance indicator reports are produced for each committee - these refer inter alia to the plan targets.

Key priorities are sub divided into objectives/targets for development which forms the basis of measurable performance review system.

Each service will have a working group which will be comprised of members and officers. The group will look at service provision and then feed these ideas into the corporate planning process.

Through service plans.

Performance review sub committee looks at policy review. Policies/policy objectives are identified and effectiveness reviewed. Policy objectives will be fed into the strategic/business planning process which will be subject to performance review.

Provides information for forward planning cycle.

Each department examines the strategic objectives, through their business plans through to their own performance indicators.

Most of these responses indicate that the foundation of a structure to review performance exists but that it lacks structure or is still relatively embryonic. A number of chief executives reported *ad hoc* reviews of particular service areas being undertaken, normally in response to something being amiss.

Respondents were asked whether a review system had been in place in the past and if so why it was no longer operational. Seventeen (15.6 per cent) reported that a review system had been in place in the past. A complete set of responses is given in Box P.

Box P: Why is your review system no longer operational?

It was abandoned many years ago on the grounds that little notice was taken of the results and the basis was inappropriate. The system was extremely badly designed and was too centralised.

The system collapsed for a number of reasons but predominately because of the lack of credibility which the system operated in this authority had, which may reflect the inadequacies of the system rather than of performance review as such.

Too broad.

System collapsed.

Very loose arrangements through a performance review sub-committee was ineffective and the system lapsed 10 years ago.

Pressure of external change.

Change in leadership and chief executive.

Discounted many years ago when the performance review sub-committee exceeded its powers.

Fell into disrepute because of complexity.

There was a change in the chief executive and the new one considered that the performance review system consisted of no more than a position statement on various services which was barely given a glance by committees. It was achieving nothing.

This was many years ago and it failed.

A formal system was introduced by a previous chief executive but did not operate satisfactorily.

A performance review committee was disbanded because it tended to review departmental reports of performance and not performance itself.

Rewards produced by the system exceeded our financial resource.

Lacked meaningful performance indicators.

This was abandoned in the early 1980s. It was considered centrally prescriptive in an authority with strong service departments and members' support was insufficient.

Committee structures were simplified with the task specifically allotted to service committees. Each committee draws up a committee plan at the start of the year (with increasing emphasis placed on performance indicators in line with Audit Commission proposals) and considers a monitoring report regularly against these. No longer centrally managed but system still operating.

Reasons for discontinuing performance review are wide ranging and a recurrent theme is that the system failed some years back. Some of the review systems which had previously been in operation are reported as being too centralist but complexity is also highlighted. A mention is made of inability to generate meaningful performance indicators.

Council leaders were asked about what factors might be inhibiting the introduction of a performance review system in their authorities. A set of the responses achieved is given in Box Q.

Box Q: What factors are inhibiting the introduction of performance review in your authority?

Cost to a small authority.

Never been considered.

Extensive legislation.

The Accounts Commission Citizen's Charter proposals adequately address the issue of performance measurement for this authority.

Development of objectives.

Too busy with CCT.

Satisfied with existing arrangement.

Previous failure.

Corporate strategy incomplete.

Staff input since they are already overworked.

Financial pressures (capping etc.) have forced us to axe our performance review team.

Other priorities and the need to establish a system of committee targets as a preliminary step towards the introduction of a performance review system.

Time and resources.

None, system not desired.

A number of these responses stress the resource implications of introducing and operating a performance review system with the cost to a small authority cited by one authority and others indicating that so much time and resources were concentrated on legislative changes particularly CCT. A number of responses indicated that the authority was quite satisfied with its current arrangement. Previous failures were also inhibiting factors.

Potential future developments

Chief executives were asked about prospects for future introduction of a performance review system.

Around 68 per cent of those questioned felt that such a system would be introduced in the future. On the other hand, 24 per cent responded negatively to this question.

Leaders were also questioned about this kind of issue. Most felt that there would be party and officer support for such a development and overall around 65 per cent expected to see a performance review system during the lifetime of their administrations.

Summing up

In this chapter we have obtained a broad overview of issues surrounding the development and operation of performance review systems in British local government. More detailed insights were obtained from the case study work and these are reported in the next chapter. The following chapter will then draw conclusions from both chapters taken together.

6 Performance review: case studies

The use of case study evidence

The survey data that we have gathered in the previous Chapter is very valuable in giving us an overview of performance review activity in British local authorities. Sometimes, however, we can gain further insights by the use of case studies in which we study in much more detail the experience of a number of individual authorities.

This also has an advantage from the research perspective. Denzin (1978) has argued that:

> Because each method reveals different aspects of empirical reality multiple methods of observation must be employed. This is termed triangulation. I offer as a final methodological rule the principle that multiple methods should be used in every investigation.
> (Denzin, 1978, p28)

Patton also describes methodological triangulation as the use of multiple methods to solve a single problem or program (1980, p109).

Case study research is defined by Hartley (1994) as:

> Case study research consists of a detailed investigation, often with data collected over a period of time of one or more organisations, or groups within organisations, with a view to providing an analysis of context and processes involved in the phenomenon under study.
> (Hartley, 1994, p208)

Although case study research allows detailed investigation of individual authorities, there are clearly worries about the extent to which one particular case can be generalised.

As Bryman (1988) has observed:

> For many people reliance on a single case poses a problem about how far it is possible to generalise the results of such research ... Many display an unease about the extent to which their findings are capable of generalisation beyond the confines of the particular case.
>
> (Bryman, 1988, p88)

A potential solution to this problem could be to take more than one case and to ensure that the cases represented a wide range of different institutions and circumstances.

Yin (1994) lists various kinds of evidence that can be used to obtain information from case studies. These are documentation, archival records, interviews, direct observation, participant observation and physical artefacts.

In the context of this study, physical artefacts and archival records did not exist and therefore had to be excluded as a source of evidence. The nature of review systems and resource constraints meant that observation, both direct and participant, was highly unfeasible. Consequently, documentation and interviews were used to gather information in the authorities chosen.

Procedure

It was fairly easy to obtain relevant documentation relating to their performance review systems from case study authorities. In requesting interviews, however, a decision had to be made about who should be requested to be interviewed. Chief executives and council leaders had been involved in the survey and clearly they were key players who should be involved in the interviews. It was also felt that the officer responsible for performance review could provide valuable in-depth insight into the operation of the system. Since the cooperation of directors of service departments was essential in the successful operation of a performance review system, an interview was requested with such a service director. In addressing the political dimension of performance review it was felt also appropriate to interview the leader or senior member of an opposition party. Interviews can be of different types:

1   In *standard* or *structured* interviews the wording of the questions and the order in which they are asked are the same from one interview to another. This is the approach used by market researchers.

2   In the *semi structured* interview, the interviewer asks certain major questions in the same way each time but is forced to alter their sequence and probe for more information. The interviewer can thus adapt the research instrument to the level of understanding of the respondent.

3   Finally, in the *unstructured* or *focused* interview interviewers have a list of topics which they wish to talk about but the interview takes place in what is almost a conversational mode.

The semi-structured interview seemed most appropriate for this research since we have already identified a number of issues which we wish to investigate further.

The authorities which were involved in the performance review case studies are as follows:

1   Authority A - English District Council.
2   Authority B - London Borough.
3   Authority C & D - County Councils in England.

The presentation of each case study will be as follows:

1   Description of the performance review system.
2   Where relevant, discussions from relevant documentation supplied by the participating authority.
3   Key issues from interviews.
4   Critique of each case in the light of the above evidence.

Case study: Authority A

The performance review system

The introduction of performance review into authority A was closely associated with the appointment of a new chief executive to the authority. Prior to this, committees had routinely received financial statistics and general management information, normally determined by chief officers. The new chief executive felt a need to make the authority much more strategic.

The development of a performance review system was seen as an essential part of this process. It was argued that 'monitoring and review simply stated, is the means by which the council can measure its success in meeting its objectives'.

Authority A's strategy was based on five corporate goals. These were as follows:

Economic viability - Particularly by promoting diversity in the economy by encouraging established industries to remain and attracting new non-land intensive industries.

Quality of environment - Preservation of the environment by investment in conservation, statutory protection, education and lobbying. Minimise pollution, litter, physical deterioration and encourage community pride.

Excellence in housing provision - Involving managing and maintaining of the council's own housing to high standards; increasing provision of affordable and social housing for rent or ownership in cooperation with the independent and private sectors; and possibly encouraging the renovation of sub-standard and private housing.

Cultural and recreational opportunities - Extend and improve cultural and recreational activities for all sections of the community and promote participation by residents and visitors.

Relations with the community - Respond to needs of the public (both residents and visitors) more effectively, especially the disabled and isolated groups. Identify the resources available within the community and develop them.

The next step in generating a performance review system in authority A was to cascade these corporate objectives into a set of service objectives. This was done in a further document. The service objectives of every committee have been brought together in this document to reflect the council's *corporate* work and vision; to improve *communication* and understanding both inside and outside the council; to ensure that *connections* were made between council objectives and to ensure a *consistency* of approach. Finally, this was a document which will be available to everyone to *consult*.

For example, we saw the following objectives set for the refuse collection service:

1   To provide and maintain an efficient and cost-effective refuse collection service ensuring that the contractor complies with specified schedules.
2   To operate the service to the satisfaction of the general public.
3   To review level, quality and method of refuse collection prior to retendering; including the possible introduction of wheelie bins and a kerbside collection service.

It was not explained, however, how these service objectives related back to the corporate ones.

The authority had produced documents about the derivation of appropriate performance indicators. It maintained that these should be directly linked to stated service objectives. In some instances, targets should also be set but in many cases a record of performance needed to be established in order to accurately gauge a realistic target.

For refuse collection the following indicators were employed:

1   Missed collections/complaints as a percentage of total service.
2   Failed inspection by cleansing inspector as percentage of inspections.
3   Missed collections remedied within one working day (target 100%).
4   Cost comparison of service with other local authorities as a percentage of average cost (when supplied by Audit Commission).

5   Review service and prepare documents for retendering.

Overall, however, the documentation did not provide a clear description of the system or why it was designed in the way it was. The role of officers and members were clearly laid out.

Interviews at authority A

Interview with officers with performance review responsibilities

The performance review section consisted of a head, two senior performance review officers and an assistant performance review officer. Its main function was 'to measure the council's success in meeting its stated objectives and obtaining value for money', and much of its activity was focused on conducting workshops that introduced performance review to officers and members, in assisting service managers to develop appropriate performance indicators and also in conducting *ad hoc* in-house reviews and customer surveys.

The interview with the head of this section confirmed that the chief executive had been the driving force behind the introduction of performance review to the authority. Unfortunately, however, he was unable to take all his chief officers with him.

> The chief executive assumed that because he was keen on this idea, that his chief officers were also - this was not always the case. Whilst a few were enthusiastic, many were indifferent, viewing this as a 'vague' technique and a few were hostile and suspicious. I did do some seminars in an attempt to secure participation but I don't think I was given enough time or legitimacy to do this properly.

The interviewee was, however, encouraged by the feeling that support was increasing rather than dwindling and some who were once indifferent were now keen supporters.

With regard to members, a special review sub-committee was set up to lead the initiative and the interviewee gave a presentation demonstrating the uses of performance review. She felt that currently:

> Some members participate in the special review sub-committee but I suspect that many still do not understand the full value of performance review and the potential that it has to offer them in terms of informed decision making. However, none have been obstructive in any way but a few have been lukewarm.

This officer complained that she seems 'to have to try to persuade people of the value of performance review rather than advocating its usefulness in authority A'. This remark, perhaps, reflects the way the system was set up without gaining the necessary degree of ownership, commitment and enthusiasm. Her view was that the system would be unlikely to collapse whilst the current chief executive remained in post but 'in his absence, I don't think that it is sufficiently embedded into the organisation to guarantee its long term viability'.

She also felt that insufficient account was taken of organisational culture:

> The culture of the organisation was not ready for performance management. I think in a way we went too fast. If we had gone more slowly then perhaps it would more readily have been absorbed into the authority.

The main strengths of the system were considered to be the following:

> I think it has provided us with information that we can understand and has supplied those people making decisions with relevant information. It has provided a fresh way of looking at service areas and has, I think, moved us towards thinking more of our customer needs and of the standard of service required. Our clients do not need a Rolls Royce service but they need something reliable. It's about matching demand with supply.

In assessing its weaknesses, she reported:

> If you're not careful, it can become too complicated and can lose its focus. Performance review is not an end in itself and there is a danger that reviewing performance will occur as a matter of course but without changing anything. Its limitations must be recognised. In this authority it is too early to specify other weaknesses but I suspect, that in time, it will be used for political purposes by senior managers bidding for resources as well as councillors of differing political persuasions. I hope political purposes do not dominate.

The interviewee considered that it would be premature to conclude whether or not performance review had been successful but proposed that:

> In the final analysis, if chief officers perceive performance review to be a useful tool then they will use it. If not, they won't. I think we have some way to go on this front.

It is clear from this remark that the review system was considered to be mainly a management tool with the evidence suggesting that it may have been perceived by these managers of questionable benefit.

There is no doubt that the chief executive considered himself to be the instigator of the performance review system. He felt, that prior to his appointment, the authority lacked vision and strategic direction. Establishing the review unit was part of his effort to make the council more strategic. Nevertheless, he found some resistance to these changes:

> The biggest difficulty was the general resistance from the bureaucracy to a new initiative or fundamental change. Many officers were uncomfortable with a system which could potentially criticise them and there was difficulty in getting recognition that performance review is more about getting feedback than criticism. Any criticism that does come out is constructive. It marks the progress towards goals and demonstrates achievements. Some chief officers felt it was an attempt at improving big brother's ability to watch over them. Officers had to be forced to stand back and see that it was an attempt to rationalise service delivery and recognise that performance review is not about criticising the past. It is about moving into the future.

Departmental progress varied because of differences in effectiveness of chief officers. In some cases 'animosity' was encountered. This respondent, however, saw the need for greater ownership of the performance review system:

> On the people front I would like to feel that everyone saw the relevance of performance review and were enthusiastic. They should require less help and support in developing and operating the system.

When asked about his views of the success of the system, he responded:

> The performance review system has contributed to changing the culture of the authority. It has helped make activities more focused and facilitated officers having a clearer idea of future targets. The organisation, as a result, is more strategic.

Its main strengths were:

> It clarifies what activities people are doing and why. It brings greater meaning to their work and makes them realise what bit of the jigsaw they are and how the whole thing fits together. It leads to better quality decision making and better quality/more informed complaints.

Its main weaknesses were:

It is open to abuse. It places an undue emphasis on trust in developing meaningful and not misleading performance indicators. There is a tendency for it to be repetitive so it is difficult to keep fresh but if it is to be successful then it cannot be static.

Overall, the strong impression was gained from this interview, that at authority A performance review was largely a management tool and that the role of elected members in this process was marginal.

Interview with chair of special review sub committee

At the time of the interview the Conservatives were the largest party and effectively the ruling group.
Asked about his party's disposition towards the introduction of performance review he stated:

> We were the largest party but to be quite honest we had some doubts and I, particularly, was quite cynical. I have been a councillor for 24 years and I've seen quite a few initiatives in my time, none of which have survived or have added anything to the organisation. However, whilst I wouldn't say we were supportive of its introduction, the chief executive was very enthusiastic and most chief officers seemed keen so we were not obstructive. My reaction is fairly typical but some of the younger members, particularly those that work in the public sector, were more favourably disposed towards performance review.

Such an apathetic attitude from a councillor who effectively has responsibility for the performance review system was disturbing. He also reinforces certain points about lack of member involvement suggesting that the system is 'mainly officer driven, demanding very little input from members'. Although members were consulted about the introduction of performance review, they 'were not involved in the creation of the system' although 'accepting the adequacy of what has evolved'.
Furthermore, the little member involvement that did occur is largely reactive:

> Member involvement is really confined to looking at targets and indicators etc. which go before service committees annually.

The strategic focus of the authority was then investigated. Responses on the subject suggested that policies tended to emerge rather than be formally developed. It seemed that officers are then supposed to assimilate them:

> I suppose our policies are widely known in the authority and it is up to officers to take them on board when organising their department's

activities and setting indicators and targets. If there was any suggestion or evidence at committees that policies were being ignored then we would rapidly take action.

This respondent did concede that linkages between the performance review system and policy planning process should be tightened up. He argued, however, that it would not be appropriate to make such a linkage with the budgetary process since 'performance review is for management but the budgetary process is political'. This is the kind of response that might be expected from a finance driven authority.

When asked what he regarded the main strengths of the system to be he responded:

> It offers the opportunity of proving that things are cost effective. If it can prove that certain activities are done because they need to be done and not just because they have always been done or are too difficult to stop doing, then this will be a strength. Its success is dependent on there being the will throughout the organisation to use it and get the most out of the system.

The following response was obtained on the main weakness:

> The weakness will be in the human element and how certain individuals respond. At present, it is too quantitatively driven and I'm not sure of its ability to answer specific questions, for example, why was there a queue at the sports centre? Not all of the measures are meaningful, for example, the number of tourists visiting the baths does not tell us anything about the performance of the attendance staff at the baths.

This response perhaps reflected a failure to communicate one of the most important roles of performance review which is to raise questions and to suggest areas where further exploration might be necessary.

Future developments suggested included the linking of performance review to staff appraisal.

Interview with service director

In this case an interview was carried out with the director of housing. This department had had to produce service performance indicators for a number of years and thus had a closer relationship with performance review issues.

This officer was much less bullish about performance review than the earlier interviewees. In his view the authority was 'a long way from having such a system up and running - we are only at the very early stages'.

This was quite discouraging, particularly as this respondent considered that the housing department was more advanced than other sections of the council because it had been required to produce statutory performance information for some time.

Even within housing, however, there were different rates of progress amongst units:

> Once the service objectives have been agreed at committee, it is left to officers to determine and use performance measures to assess progress towards targets and less specific service objectives - members are not involved in the monitoring process. Most unit managers in housing have used the legislative indicators as the basis for this, but a few sections have worked with the review unit to devise meaningful and appropriate performance indicators. This is indicative of the preliminary stage that we are at - even within housing there is not a consistent approach.

He also felt that there have been considerable differences in standards of service objectives and performance indicators set for service areas throughout this council because this was left to the discretion of officers. Nevertheless, the system has tended to make member decision making more strategic and to make officers more disciplined:

> Performance review and particularly service objectives have been very useful at pinning down members to clearly think about what they want and to be more strategic in decision making. The mechanical process of reporting to committee and producing performance review information will help directors sharpen up.

On the other hand, however, there have been certain negative outcomes. These included excessive bureaucracy, paperwork and the fact that the system 'ignored many aspects of service delivery which were difficult to measure'.

Many of the problems that are outlined appear to be associated with the lack of ownership felt by officers towards performance review:

> The idea of service objectives being produced and associated performance information being generated has been centrally imposed ... I think the chief executive who has driven the introduction of the process should have consulted with chief officers and members much more. If he had, I think we would perceive that we own the system much more and would not feel it had been imposed. It would also have effected a much needed change in culture. If consultation had occurred, then I think the system would be different because our needs would have been recognised and we would have defined a different role for performance review. Many of us have useful experience that could have been drawn on.

A further problem outlined is that the performance review team were marketed as watchdogs so directors were reluctant to allow them into their departments. Also, there seemed to be a lack of clarity about what the role of the team should be. He also drew attention to the lack of clear corporate goals, and a compartmentalised approach to service delivery. Once such corporate goals were established, then he felt that performance review would help to facilitate their achievement.

Nevertheless, too many people at authority A were lukewarm towards the performance review process:

> I don't think we have the correct climate to do meaningful performance review since this requires the officers collectively to be supportive of each other so that we can openly discuss failings and problems in achieving objectives. We can't really go to members for discussion on aspects of review. They don't really understand the process and are not particularly supportive of the initiative.

Finally, there was still a problem with perception of the system:

> Still seen by some [performance review system], if not many, as a stick to beat officers with and the performance review unit a watchdog generating the lethal information.

Interview with opposition leader

The interviewee was with the main opposition party leader (in this case the Liberal Democrats). When the system was introduced the Liberal Democrats were supportive because they saw it as a means of identifying opportunities for improving efficiency and making savings. Like the housing director, however, he felt that performance review has not been fully implemented and would like to see the current system overhauled.

He confirmed that members had little input to the development of the system and that little information feeds through to members beyond the indicators and measures presented annually to service committees. In any case, he believed that such indicators 'only scratch the surface'.

He believed that the role taken by the special review sub committee was to 'look at *ad hoc* issues rather than the systematic monitoring of performance' and that the committee lacks power and is 'officer driven'. The lack of policy direction was attributable to the 'steady as you go - don't rock the boat attitude of the majority group'.

The need to link the budgetary and planning processes to the performance review process was recognised. A recurring theme in this interview was the inadequacies of the indicators used. This 'affords us little opportunity for changing things in this authority'.

Performance review in authority A: a critique

We can see from the above that there seemed to be considerable problems with performance review at authority A. It is clear from the interviews that performance review was considered only a management tool, but a primary problem appeared to be a lack of ownership from managers who should be using it. Interviews with members suggested lack of commitment, enthusiasm and understanding of the purposes and potential of performance review. There were also undertones of a watchdog culture in operation. Although on the positive side, all interviewees were able to identify some strengths in the review system, it was clear that the council was nowhere near achieving its potential.

It is worthwhile considering what lessons can be derived from the above case. We would tentatively postulate that the following may be key problems:

1   The council's lack of a strategic perspective. There seemed to be no clear policy making process with the consequence that policies 'emerge' and were unclear. The interview with the deputy leader of the majority group suggested very much a finance driven council. It is difficult to develop an effective system for reviewing performance if we do not have clear goals which we wish to achieve.

2   It is clear from the interviews that the performance review system was virtually imposed on the council by the chief executive as part of his attempt to make the council's policy making more strategic. The interviews suggested that insufficient attention was paid to gaining ownership of both officers and members. It was apparently hoped that the introduction of the performance review system would by itself help to develop a more strategic culture. Many would argue that was the wrong way round; if a more strategic culture has been developed, then performance review may help us implement this change.

3   The lack of ownership, commitment and involvement by members makes the future prospects for the system very uncertain.

4   Although the performance review section published useful advice on developing performance indicators some respondents were unhappy about the appropriateness of indicators developed. A further problem may be the system of cascading service objectives. This did not appear to be associated with any service planning work which might outline how objectives might be delivered. Such a system might exacerbate problems of developing effective performance review.

Case study : Authority B

Case study authority B is a London Borough which at the time of the interviews was Labour controlled and had a population of around 250,000. There are two modes of performance review in this authority:

1   Through undertaking reviews of specific aspects of service delivery. Such *ad hoc* reviews were particularly common during a period when the council faced financial crisis over an extended period of time. During this period the council decided to eliminate what they regarded as less essential activities rather than impose steep cuts across the board. These reviews were still performed under the auspices of the finance department although major efforts have been made to lose 'the hatchet man image'.

2   The second approach to performance review emerged from service programmes. These programmes were developed as a response to dissatisfaction with the council's performance, particularly the gap between policies and perceived performance and its inability to respond quickly and imaginatively. At this time the authority found the mental model developed by the local government training board of particular value .

This model distinguished between 'closed' and 'open' authorities. The distinction between the two types of authority is given below.

Closed authority	**Open authority**
Bureaucratic and slow	Responsive/action based
Inward looking	Outward looking
Inaccessible	Accessible
Hierarchical	Flexible
Unfriendly	Delegating authority
Preoccupied with administration and systems	Concerned about people

At this time the authority identified itself as 'closed' but wanted to change to become 'open'.

The transformation began with a discussion of the general direction in which the council was moving and agreement on the following core values:

Putting services to the public first This should involve consultation to ensure that appropriate services are provided, being responsible, flexible and making the best use of resources.

Local government serving local communities Particularly by giving them some influence over what happens in the borough.

Equal opportunities for the people of borough B Recognising inequalities and taking action to reduce them.

Taking action to be more efficient and effective

Valuing employees Valuing the whole of the workforce and expecting managers to give the necessary support and direction. Aiming for quality.

Caring for the environment Influencing and regulating others to make the borough a cleaner and greener place. Services should make the best use of limited resources and protect and enhance the natural and built environment.

The next step was for departments to draw up service plans/programmes that embraced these core values. Service plans are four year development plans for the service, whereas programmes are an annual plan.

Service programmes have to identify key result areas, relevant targets and appropriate measures of success for reporting twice per year. The central policy unit oversees the drawing up of the plan and ensures that it has secured the approval of the relevant committee. There is no mechanism for central coordination or the subsequent reporting of performance. This reflects authority B's strong emphasis on devolved management, a consequence of which is considerable variation of effort and detail.

An employee development scheme has evolved from the core value of 'valuing employees'. Key tasks/objectives are agreed for each member of staff in discussion with his/her manager. Actions required to perform these tasks are identified together with associated training needs. It is implicitly assumed, of course, that the key tasks/objectives for individual staff members reflect each department's service plan.

Documentation

A wide range of documentation is available including both service programme and service development plan for leisure services. As mentioned above, there is a four year development plan for the service area.

The service development plan consists of the following sections:

Changing needs, diminishing resources

This includes discussion of relevant legislative changes, budgetary reductions, future leisure needs and considers future demographic, socio-economic and political changes.

Which examines the current position and priority of each area of service (e.g. library, outdoor recreation etc.), and considers priorities for the next planning period.

Strategy for success

Strategies take account of demographic, social, economic and technological changes outlined and identified in the first section and priorities identified in the previous section. Particular attention is given to enabling, providing individual quality experiences within mass provision, equality of access, relevance to community needs.

Planning into practice

Suggests ways in which the strategy developed in the previous section can be put into practice.

The *service programme* begins by applying the core values to leisure services. For each area it describes the background to the service, overall service aims, targets (and their associated core values) and measures of success. An example is produced below with respect to a theatre in authority B.

Example - theatre in authority B

Background to service

Theatre B attracts almost 135,000 annually for a diverse range of events and performances. Its customers are drawn from a wide cross section of the community, which also reflects the council's target groups. Service standards have recently been published and the aim is to constantly improve on these standards.

Overall service aim

To provide an efficient and effective service to all audiences. The following are examples of the targets set for this service (note there are, in fact, eight in all).

Table 6.1
Targets set for theatre service

Targets to achieve	Core values to achieve		Measures of success
Increase audiences' target from 135,000 to 138,000 during the year.	LG, PS	(a)	Achievement of target of 138,000.
Increase the attendance by black people to attendances 23,500 (from 21,400) representing a minimum of 17% of total.	EO, PS, LG	(b)	Achievement of target of 23,500 attendances.
Double the number to ten and extend the range of signed performances for customers with hearing difficulties.	PS, AQ	(c)	Achievement of target of ten signed performances.

Core values legend PS - putting services to the public first; LG - local government serving local people; EO - equal opportunities; AQ - aiming for quality.

It can be seen that the service programmes are very similar to what other authorities may call action plans.

Interviews at authority B

At authority B it was impossible to arrange an interview with a representative of minority groups who refused to cooperate. Since the council is completely dominated by Labour who hold eighty five percent of the seats, the influence of the minority group, however, is likely to be marginal.

Interview with officer with performance review responsibilities

Interviews were carried out with officers who were responsible for both the service planning work and for the in depth reviews.
They identified the origin of performance review in their authority:

Performance review has emerged from the continued fiscal crises that faced the authority throughout the 1980s. The in-depth reviews were helping us to identify what could be done better in specific areas and was assisting with the rationalisation of cuts. However, we were beginning to lose sight of our overall purpose and the introduction of service programmes, which forced departments to consider their purpose, was a way of addressing this.

Unlike authority A, this initiative was originally proposed by members, particularly the deputy leader of policy, although its introduction was subsequently driven by officers.

Members were enthusiastic and at one stage had set up a member performance review working group to undertake reviews of particular service areas. Although very productive, it required so much effort that it was not repeated on anything like the same scale. 'Now member involvement varies depending on the service area they are involved in and how developed performance review is in that service area'.

As far as officers were concerned we learnt that the original scrutiny system, which was really a cost-cutting exercise, caused a great deal of resentment. By the time that the authority began work on the service programming area a much better relationship had emerged.

There is inter-relationship between the two performance review systems because if the service programmes indicated problematic areas then they would become candidates for a future in-depth scrutiny.

Authority B has a high level of departmental delegation, although the review officers felt that more consistency in approach across departments would be advantageous. 'This would be done at the risk of the centre having to interfere'. Possibly this might jeopardise all progress made to date.

These officers felt that there was a need to try to coordinate policy better, probably by introducing council objectives in addition to the core values:

We are traditionally compartmental here and this has been reinforced by the prolonged fight for resources between departments so I think we would benefit from a collective statement of authority B's objectives, but as yet we do not have one.

In fact, one of the weaknesses reported of the performance review process in authority B is that 'it has reinforced compartmentalism, the remoteness of the authority's departments from one another'. Devolved management had allowed those chief officers who did not really want to bother with performance review to do the minimum. Nevertheless, it had also given progressive managers a tool to demonstrate all they are achieving with their resources and to highlight what could be achieved with additional amounts.

In summary, the main strengths of the process were identified as:

It has helped authority B face successive government challenges, particularly on the financial front. It has helped us rationalise cuts and has assisted in our devolved management system. It has instilled a sense of what is a good manager. Because of our very small central core, authority B is dominated by professionalism but I think the review system has identified some issues which were previously considered to not be of relevance in service departments. The change in culture which has slowly taken place owes a lot to the operation of service programming. Defining a set of core values and getting officers to link their targets and indicators to them is progress in itself.

Interview with assistant chief executive

The assistant chief executive is responsible for the central policy unit which oversees the process under which the very limited central coordination required at authority B is carried out:

> The only central coordination of the programme is through a check on each department's service programme. Beyond this, it is up to committee chairs to make sure that they are receiving the relevant information twice a year and that the department has implemented the service programme as envisaged.

He acknowledged that the introduction of the performance review initiative did not meet as much resistance as expected even though initially some chief officers suspected that it constituted an attempt by the centre to regain a foothold.

Performance review at authority B was, he suggested:

> Really just an activity to support policy implementation ... a mechanism for ensuring that officers follow through on delivery once a policy has been determined.

There was some surprise that members, whose profile was relatively young, had not demanded a wider role. Such a strengthened role could be an appropriate future development.

Training had been provided to support the introduction of service programming. All middle managers were given a training programme on core values and how these could influence service delivery. Some training in service planning was given by an external consultant. Not too much guidance was given on developing targets and indicators because it was believed that ownership would be maximised if they evolved independently.

In summary, this respondent stated that although the system at authority B appeared to be comparatively unstructured it was well suited to organisational needs. He also felt that the authority had been given back its sense of purpose that had been eroded by the sustained financial cuts:

> We had lost sight of what we were trying to achieve as an organisation. The whole push has been toward looking at service objectives with performance review being a mechanism for ensuring that we do not just go through the motions of setting objectives but rather to ensure that progress towards them is achieved.

Future developments might include making the system more rigorous and carrying out more in-depth analysis of the process of service delivery.

Interview with chair of policy and resources

This respondent was a senior member of the ruling Labour group. He reported that members were supportive of the service plans/programmes because it was a way out of the short-termism which had emerged from extreme budgeting pressure the council had to deal with in the preceding years. It was a way for authority B to become more strategic.

Like other respondents, he acknowledged that there had been a wide variation in responses across the council. Too much discretion had been given to chief officers and there was a need 'to find a way of retaining our devolved management system but securing a more coherent and consistent approach. However, he considered that:

> Officers at a general level have responded well, but this authority is still traumatised from the effects of the past few years and I think many are just beginning to stop operating on a reactionary basis and considering what service programmes might offer authority B.

Like other respondents, he felt that B's approach reinforced compartmentalism and that a level above the service programme defining what the council wanted to achieve corporately should be introduced. The budgetary system was basically incremental in authority B. Nevertheless:

> Although service programmes are unrelated to the budgetary provision at council level, most departments are prioritising their resource allocation on the basis of the key results areas agreed by service committees.

For the future he identified a need to take a thorough look at the contents of service programmes to assess whether these meet the actual needs of the people of authority B.

This interview was given by the director of leisure services. He was favourably disposed to the introduction of performance review:

> I was completely behind the introduction of service programming and performance review to authority B. Being a relatively small, non essential department, I have had to bear more than my fair share of the budget cuts that have faced the council during the past years. This has forced me to take a fundamental look at the services provided by this department and to prioritise accordingly and to ensure that we squeeze as much out of each pound as possible.

Nevertheless, he perceived a real division in attitudes towards service programming between professionally dominated departments such as education and social work and others such as his own which he believed to be 'more innovative and which bring people together from a range of different backgrounds and who have a bias for action'.

His view was that the highly delegated nature of performance review activity allowed some departments to do very little or 'just go through the motions whilst others take the whole process very seriously'. Within his own department the service programming approach has provided the framework to determine policies and focus on their implementation.

Overall, he felt that the authority was no longer just reacting to everything that confronted it and was becoming more strategic. Service programmes were helping to stabilise departmental agendas.

In terms of future development, he felt that there was a need to strengthen corporate identity, address what the role of the centre had now actually become, incorporate qualitative data into their system and become less London based in seeking out good practice. He also felt that there was a need for members to be more closely involved in the process in the future.

Critique of performance review in authority B

Looking at the materials and interviews obtained on authority B, the overall impression is that the system has been operated relatively successfully. Both strands of the performance review system had been developed in response to perceived needs. The in-depth review system had been initially employed to identify areas for cuts but had later been used for investigating possible problem areas. The system that was associated with the service programmes had developed to counter a situation where years of budget cuts had made the authority short-termist and unfocused. The following issues may well be significant:

1   As mentioned above, the systems were adopted as the result of perceived needs and were supported by both members and officers. Indeed, it seems that it was proposed by members. This, together with meaningful consultation, contributed to ownership of the system by all concerned.
2   Expectations for the system appeared to be realistic. It was expected that the system would help to strengthen the strategic position of the council but would take a period of time.
3   Technically the performance review system was tied to the system of service programmes which themselves were part of the four year service planning system. Thus, the performance review system was completely integrated with the policy planning system.
4   Most respondents identified the 'compartmentalism' of departments as a major problem. Management delegation to service committees had led to a balkanised structure with a loss of corporate perspectives. In the planning system the values of the council lead directly to the service plans/programmes. There was a need to develop a more corporate perspective and this might involve at least setting organisation-wide-objectives.

Case study: Authority C

This case is an English County Council. This performance review system emerged from a major review of council activities conducted by external consultants. The terms of reference for the consultants' study required proposals that:

1   Shifted the focus of the organisation towards meeting customer needs.
2   Enables members to better agree their political objectives.
3   ensures that changes to management arrangements result in improved and efficient service delivery.

The consultants' report contained a statement of corporate principles and proposals for a member structure and officer machinery. (Figure 6.1) The new committee structure would need to:

1   Help members focus on strategy and policy making (an area which members felt needed improvement).
2   Increase efficiency in the use of officer and member time.
3   allow members to concentrate on what they are best at (i.e. articulating constituency views, deciding policy, assessing performance).
4   Let managers manage (i.e. decreasing member involvement in day to day operational decisions).
5   Be outward facing, emphasising customer needs.

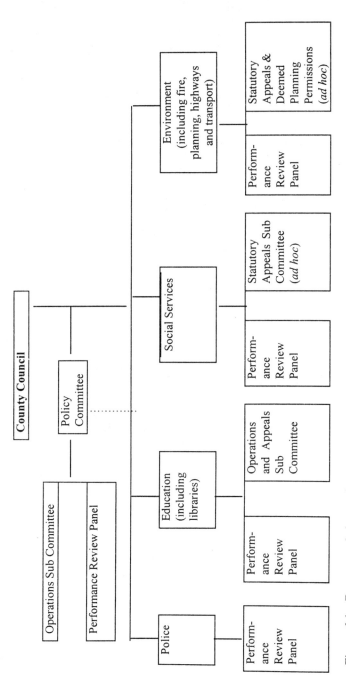

Figure 6.1 Recommended committee structure

This structure includes a simplified arrangement of four service committees which within the framework laid down by the policy committee have freedom to determine service policy and to allocate resources (this proposal drastically reduces the numbers of committees and sub-committees found in the previous structure). Another important innovation is that each of the service committees have attached performance panels with responsibility for 'monitoring and evaluating' the associated service committees. The consultants' report suggests that review panels should include members with an independent and objective view of performance as well as committee members who have experience of the particular service area. It is recommended that the vice chair of the service committee but NOT the chair should be a member of the panel. A major issues agenda would need to be determined between the service committees and the panel and a formal reporting mechanism established. Thus what is being proposed is a strongly *member based* system.

The consultants also suggest changes to the officer machinery. It is proposed that this change begins at chief officer level and subsequently cascades down through all the other levels of an organisation. The objective of the change would be to align the business plan with job responsibilities, personal objectives and the reward system.

Documentation

A wide range of documentation was supplied by authority C. These included a newsletter entitled 'Performance Review News' where it was reported that both the District Auditor and the Audit Commission felt that C's approach to performance review was one of the most radical in the country.

It was clear from looking at past agendas that panels work by selecting a range of important issues rather than reviewing performance comprehensively, say through the use of service plan mechanisms. For example, a review of a police performance review panel revealed that the following issues were under consideration:

1   Motor car crime - paper supplying information on the extent of motor car crime.
2   Police authority housing - investigating the effectiveness with which the police housing stock was being managed.
3   Report on police complaints and their handling.
4   A report suggesting ways of reviewing police performance.

Interviews at authority C

Interview with officer with performance review responsibilities

This interview revealed that prior to the introduction of the current system a performance review system based on a performance review sub-committee (a sub-committee of policy and resources) had existed. This system was described as 'undoubtedly internal, organisationally based and focused on what we did and how we did it'.

Authority C was 'now seeking to be much more strategic in its approach, shifting from operational details towards the broader policy dimension'. In particular, the role of members within performance review was significantly enhanced because it was claimed that the system operated in this authority was about the review of policies.

The review panels associated with the new system were to have a wider scope for action:

> We want them to be persistent, curious, independent and thorough. We want them to be investigative and, thus have, sought to give them a high level of freedom. Centralist intervention and demands would, I think, stifle innovation and ultimately their operation and they would fade into the background. Their responsibilities are clear but how they meet these is at their discretion.

To some, however, this wider discretion might be seen as a weakness:

> Some of our members feel insecure about not receiving tons of data on performance and I think we are at risk of succumbing to pressure and becoming paper driven in our approach to review. If this happens, I think it will become a mundane exercise and achieve nothing. They have struggled with a role which really is about testing things intellectually as opposed to mechanically.

There has been some criticism that it took a long time to implement the system. The pace of implementation was constrained by the need to keep both members and officers 'on board'. In fact, some members were originally suspicious that the new system was a ploy for pushing them to the periphery rather than the opposite.

The system was regarded as still evolving which has resulted in some frustration being felt by officers who were hoping for more immediate change:

> Those officers and members that think it is working think it is a wonderfully powerful tool, but in order to be successful that core group of believers needs to be widened. I suppose it has changed some of the things that we do and the way that we do them and has required officers to be

more explicit about what they think the policies are that they are responsible for delivering. Thus, members have had to clarify what their policies are. This is quite a significant achievement but needs to be sustained and built upon.

Nevertheless, it was felt that the performance review system was gradually changing the roles of members of the authority, 'forcing them to become policy orientated'.

Future important developments were considered to be raising the profile of performance review even further, making 'those involved in its operation feel that they are making an important contribution'. It was proposed that this could be partially done by providing more training and workshops for members 'to enhance their understanding of the process'. It would also be appropriate to seek greater consistency of approach between the review panels.

Although the authority has stated a wish to act more strategically, there appeared to be little corporate focus. There was no mission statement or statement of objectives because each standing committee must decide its own purpose. The council has laid down four corporate principles: communication, accountability, responsiveness and enabling. Beyond this, however, it appeared to be up to each standing committee to decide its own purpose.

Interview with chief executive

The chief executive took up post towards the end of the management review which was discussed earlier. He was given the opportunity to influence the shape of the final document and was favourably disposed towards performance review seeing it as a vehicle for 'redefining the proper political role of members'. Apparently, it also took a long time to get the distinction between policy performance review and the measurement of performance of individuals clearly drawn. He considers the latter to be a managerial role.

Initially he reported 'that there were many minor difficulties such as members understanding their responsibilities and that it has felt like 'an uphill struggle to get us to where we are now'. This was particularly due to the new system 'challenging some of our traditions'. There were also problems with some of the participants in the performance review process:

> People are the biggest weakness. They have motivations which are not necessarily in accord with improving organisational performance. Additionally, we have drawn a notional line between scrutinising the performance of managers and the performance of policies. If a policy is not having the desired impact, it may be because it is being poorly implemented or it may be because it is an ill-conceived policy. It is a convenient line to draw but not altogether appropriate and I think in time we will run into problems in this domain.

He felt also that insufficient progress had been made in developing policy targets and performance indicators and this was 'hampering the effectiveness of performance review'. More resources needed to be allocated to the process and, in particular, members needed more support. However, the chief executive considered that there was a risk that the centre would take over whereas, ideally, they were only there to 'lubricate the process'. He also felt that members needed to frame their policies more coherently and he wanted to see the review panels given 'better quality members', reiterating the view that they were currently considered by councillors as 'the poor relation to the standing committees and a place for relatively junior members'.

Overall, the chief executive did not feel that performance review had been fully embedded into the organisation, with senior officers still providing the momentum and if this was removed, it was questionable whether members would continue to operate performance review in authority C.

Interview with deputy leader of the council

This interview was with the deputy leader of the council and leader of the Conservative group - the then ruling administration. Being chair of the education committee, he was consequently barred from sitting on the associated review panel. As deputy leader he was a key figure in the consultants' review and feels that what has emerged from this process does, indeed, reflect members' needs.

The purpose of the performance review panels was to 'scrutinise what the committee does, to report on the impact of relevant activities and to question whether this was what was intended'. Some policies were, however, 'so long term and vague that it is difficult to make such a link'. Most policies were inherited and only change very gradually. He felt that:

> Establishing corporate principles has been good for helping to focus on what we as an administration want to do and the whole new approach being introduced should help us as a political group determine clear policies.

Furthermore, the new framework should enable members to move away from operational issues towards more strategic considerations with the emphasis shifting to policies and outcomes and management being left to managers. Nevertheless, he believed that results would take some time to feed through and this was a cause of some dissatisfaction. More worryingly, he highlighted a serious problem associated with the membership of the review panels:

> I am concerned about the calibre of members to serve on the review panel. Some members have turned down the opportunity to serve on panels, preferring a back seat on principal committees. Whilst this continues, the review panels are not being given the best start or chance of success.

In his view it was, therefore, crucial that members' understanding of the role of review panels should improve and he would like to see members 'seeking a place on them rather than the currently dominant service committees'. It was also recognised that in the future 'we as an administration need to tighten up on the clarity of vision and expression in our policies so their implementation can be reviewed'.

Another future issue will be to get to grips with the lack of linkage between budgets and the performance review system:

> We roll forward the base budget every year with a small level of decisions taken around the margins. This is clearly something we will have to address in the future since our budget is completely divorced from our corporate principles.

Interview with service director

This interview was with the director of trading standards at authority C, who was also a lead officer in the environmental review panel. He believed performance review was only in its infancy in the authority and that 'we have only really set the framework in place, namely the review panels, and are beginning to learn how these will operate in practice, basically by doing'.

He had confidence that the review system would promote and provoke relevant questions and felt that it has a number of strengths. The extensive consultation with members at the beginning should result in 'ownership and commitment'. In addition, the lack of pressure for instant results allowed members and officers to 'feel their way through the process' and allowed the core business of the council (service delivery) to continue with minimum disruption. He believed the system fosters partnership between members and officers, encourages joint growing and learning and prevents conflict and confrontation.

However, he did recognise that the long timescale before benefits emerge may cause some frustration amongst both members and officers. He considered that members were likely to be anticipating more rapid and transparent results than was feasible. On the officer side:

> Officers will become restless, I think, if the review system and the new committee structure does not change, albeit slowly, the role which members play in the council. I actually think that down the line when officers find that review pushes them out of the driving seat and members do control strategy in their departments more, they are likely to become a little more resistant or down on the process.

He considered that members are being asked to take a huge step:

In the past it has been easier for them to be focused on the operational, the small scale details and the short term. We are asking them to become strategic, to look at the overall picture and to set policy direction for this large organisation within that. This is a big step for them to make and they need to feel that it is okay to take time to bridge the enormous gulf between the two.

He did, however, question whether there were sufficient members conversant with performance review who understood what it is all about, to actually serve on the panels.

Interview with opposition leader

This interview was with the leader of the Labour group, the largest opposition group. He reported that the decision to appoint consultants and initiate a fundamental review of council activities was undertaken without consultation with the opposition. 'This makes it difficult for us to support what has emerged even though I believe that some of the new structure may have something to offer the authority'.

Worryingly, he reported that two Labour members resigned their panel memberships because they felt too little was being achieved, particularly in connection with the lack of clear policies to review:

> I have had difficulty persuading our better members to consider taking or retaining a role on the review panels and I know that this is also the case for the Conservatives since all their front line councillors are chairs and vice chairs of the service committees.

He also believed that review will have only a short life in authority C:

> To be honest I don't think that the current system will survive because I think it will achieve too little over too long a time period. This is particularly so whilst the panels cannot attract the better quality members. Members from all the parties on the whole seem indifferent to performance and the new structure. I don't sense commitment and this does beg the question 'why bother?'. The case for performance review has not really been made. If it is to stay then I think the biggest tightening up must be a clarification of policies.

He felt that the system was just a framework and is unlikely to change the way things were done, particularly addressing the underlying problems of complacency and lack of clear policies which he felt exist in the county.

The leader was also asked whether his party would operate performance review differently, should it come to power after the next election. He responded:

If we were in power the policies would be clear and so there would be less of a problem with the existing system. I think we would need to think carefully about the role which performance should and could take and how best this could be achieved. The current system ignores the performance of officers in implementing policies and this needs to be addressed since this is a significant aspect of the performance of authority C.

He also felt that the electorate and service users have been largely ignored. If elected, they would commission views of both service users and non-users because 'we are not performing for ourselves but for them so it's only right and proper that we consult them about their views'.

Performance review in authority C: an overview

There were clearly a number of problems associated with the performance review process at authority C. It is suggested that these are associated with the following problems:

1   Lack of a clear, coherent policy framework. It is difficult to assess how far the authority's activities are achieving goals if it is unclear what these goals, in fact, are. It seems, however, that attempts are unlikely to try to rectify this situation and a number of policy panels are being set up.
2   There is evidence from the interviews of an unwillingness to undertake membership of the performance review panels. Higher calibre members appear to be attracted to the service committees. It could be that members do not fully understand the role of these committees or that they find involvement in the committees too demanding.
3   There seems to be little linkage between the policy planning process and performance review, such as the service planning process which we saw in authority B.
4   It is, of course, arguable whether it is necessarily desirable to split responsibility for service delivery and for monitoring and review in this way. It could be argued that such a split breaks the continuity of the cycle.

Thus, overall, authority C offers us an interesting member based process. Although members were consulted in setting up the process, their continued involvement may be open to doubt.

Case study: Authority D

Authority D is a large County Council with a revenue budget in excess of £1 billion. Performance review has been an important feature of its management system since local government reorganisation of 1974.

Initially, this system compromised mainly member led reviews into different areas of the authority's activity. From around the mid 1980s however the system became much more comprehensive. This led first to the development of medium term plans (a three year rolling strategic plan). This was followed by departmental business plans (equivalent to service plans) and personal action plans for each employee. We shall now consider the different elements of the planning and performance review system.

The medium term plan (MTP)

The MTP attempts to provide a clear policy direction and revenue framework for committees to operate in. It covers a three year period and is reviewed annually to take account of changing circumstances and needs and to allow the plan to be rolled forward a year. Thus, policies and resources are always projected three years ahead. Clarity over resources and policies must be combined with flexibility to allow the authority to respond to changing circumstances.

Thus, plans for post-budget years are subject to annual review and cannot be regarded as strict commitments.

The above is also combined with a base budget review process which looks critically at whether the council really needs to do all the things in its base budget. The plan is to review 20 per cent of activities each year. Thus, it can be seen that there are very strong links built in between the budgeting process and planning/performance review process.

The MTP reviews the external environment and goes on to highlight a number of key issues (or corporate priorities). Examples of these key issues are as follows:

Schools Increased investment will complete the rising fives initiative. Future years will see further investment in school buildings, maintenance and the quality of teachers.

Disadvantaged groups Substantial new investment to be made in priority areas which include children with special education needs, improving child protection and accommodating the growing numbers of elderly, handicapped and mentally ill people requiring care.

Physical environment Some increase in support for waste disposal is likely to be offset by reduction in the road and footpath maintenance programme.

Emergency services The opening of a major infrastructure project has highlighted the need for additional investment in fire and police.

The projected budgetary implications of the corporate plan are presented. As an example we shall look at the section referring to special needs.

Table 6.2
Special needs: additional expenditure

£m

		Yr 1	Yr 2	Yr 3
(a)	Special education needs-integrating children with special needs into mainstream schooling.	2.0	-	-
(b)	Child protection - responding to and dealing with the number of children being referred suffering from child abuse and implementing the Children's Act.	3.1	3.2	2.0
(c)	Community care - meeting the needs of the growing number of handicapped and mentally ill people by tailoring services to individual requirements, increasing range of day activities and transferring residential homes to the Housing Trust.	1.1	1.5	-
(d)	Services for the elderly - supporting more elderly people in their homes with 'home care' and by transferring residential homes to the Housing Trust.	0.7	0.7	0.7

In authority D the 'business planning' process is equivalent to that we have described as 'service planning' elsewhere in this volume. It is designed to translate strategic objectives agreed in the medium term plan into specific management actions for the financial year ahead. Essentially, therefore, the service plan implements the first year of the medium term plan. These plans also link the desired activity levels and performance standards in the medium term plan with actual resources available in that financial year, thus, ensuring the department has the capability to deliver the service plan. If there is a mismatch, activity levels may be adjusted or even budgets reallocated. Such adjustments would be fed back into the next year of the MTP process. Thus in summary, the business plan should set out for the year ahead:

1   What we are seeking to achieve - policy objective.
2   What resources are available, budget, buildings, manpower.
3   Desired level of activity compared against previous year - from MTP.
4   Performance level required - performance indicator.
5   Action required to achieve the desired activity and performance within the resources available.

We shall briefly look at the social service business plan. This consists of a departmental policy overview, external pressures and trends, internal responses and service policies and performance targets. This is followed by the detailed plans for each area. As an example, we shall track through the business plan for commitments with regard to elderly care.

The departmental policy overview notes that nearly 260,000 people are aged 65 or over. It is estimated that the number of elderly people in the authority, particularly over the age of 75, will continue to increase until the end of the century, further increasing the demand for services. External pressure and trends repeat the above observation and note a high incidence of dementia in the over 75s. Pressures to reduce overheads and management costs while at the same time improving financial, personnel and information support as part of devolving responsibility are increasing.

The internal response is as follows:

1   Partnership with other public, private and voluntary sectors in a 'mixed economy' of welfare provision including the transfer of some County Council residential and day care establishments the voluntary sector.
2   Providing an increased number of packages of care to meet individuals' requirements through the medium of care management. Ensuring that there is greater consumer involvement and choice, and that services are targeted to the most dependent.
3   Providing more linked service centres for Elderly people, including twenty four hour support for their carers.

The department also places considerable emphasis on its customer care policies, particularly providing information to service users; consultation, improving reception areas and service points and coordinating a rigorous an revised complaint procedure. It is planned that this will lead to the production of a consumer's charter. Regular consumer surveys are also an integral part of this initiative.

Service policies and performance targets for the elderly care are as follows (Table 6.3):

Table 6.3
Performance index

Elderly People	Indicator	Target Value for 1992/93 (1991/92 in brackets)
To increase number of elderly people cared for in own homes	Ratio of number of people in long term Council funded institutional care to the number of people receiving community care	25% (28.6%)
To target care on the most highly dependent	(a) Proportion of elderly people in Home Care scheme receiving attendance allowance	60% (60%)
	(b) proportion of elderly people receiving Council funded long-stay care who are in two high bands of dependency	46% (46%)

In addition, further performance indicators are being developed. These will include:

1   Target values for ratio of qualified staff in the department.
2   Waiting time for service provision.

More detailed plans and performance indicators are provided at the area level. Let us take one such area as an example. This contains the following service developments and performance targets.

1   Development of care management service, in line with budget increase. Target is to take on 340 new cases so that by the end of the financial year 1,940 people will be receiving such a service.
2   In order to meet the needs of elderly people who are assessed as not requiring care management, but who do require assistance to remain in their own homes, two additional rehabilitation coordinators will be appointed (making an area total of six) and a target capacity of 65 clients.
3   To increase the target capacity for day care from 225 to 380 people.

Individual action plans and resource accountability statements (RAS)

Resource accountability statements allocate cash limits and service targets to individual cost centre managers. These targets are derived directly from the business plan. Individual action plans include key objectives for the individual for the financial year. The successful delivery of targets set in the RAS will be one. Others may be more specific in nature, relating to particular parts of the process and some will be more personal, relating to training or development needs. These should all emanate from the business or medium term plan.

Progress of staff again their plan is regularly monitored and all staff qualify for performance related pay. This is based on their ratings which vary from 1 (excellent) to 5 (totally inadequate). Performance related pay may account for 6 to 10 per cent of pay.

Overview

The planning and performance review system at authority D seems to be comprehensive and strongly linked to the budgetary position. The documentation did not indicate clear vision or values however.

Interviews at authority D

With officers responsible for performance review

The current performance review system has evolved over time. It has gained the interest of members and enabled them to focus on policy rather than 'nitty gritty' issues.

The council does not have a vision or mission statement and the manifesto is not specific or visionary. There was a statement of objectives in the MTP and also a statement of managerial principles promoted by the chief executive.

Officer commitment was consolidated by a wide ranging series of management development programmes and seminars. Current programmes involved up to 1,400 managers. This officer also suggested that members had not been properly involved in the performance review process, full involvement being limited to a few chairs and the leader. Sometimes chairs have been reluctant to keep back-bench members properly informed.

To an extent, goals and targets have emerged:

> Started with many good general policy statements without much in the way of targets. More specific targets were then developed.

Performance measures and indicators are set by a wide range of people; as a general rule whoever sets the objectives sets the measures:

161

Because of the culture we do not get many projects set up without someone asking who is responsible and what we are trying to achieve.

The main problem in implementing the system was getting ownership, ensuring that people did not feel that this was something that was 'done' to them. The contracting side will see performance review as essential to their survival but this is not so immediately apparent to the client side. A further technical problem was deciding appropriate numbers of indicators:

Insufficient indicators mean that people do not appreciate what they are doing - too many results in excessive monitoring.

A feature of the performance review system was the wide involvement of staff. Overall responsibility for the process rested with the head of strategic management but major service departments also had their responsibilities for this process. A wide range of officers was involved. These include policy units (both departmental and corporate), internal audit and various external consultants who carried out work in response to commissions. In all, around 50 officers were involved in the performance review process.

The council's budgetary system was regarded by this officer as more policy led than incremental. She believed that its major strength is its close integration into management processes. Its main feature was the need to understand what level of information members actually need and whether they are getting this. Nevertheless it is believed that the authority is moving in the right direction and that the main future priority is to ensure that the system is fully bedded in.

Interview with chief executive

This interview took place with a senior policy officer who was able to represent the chief executive's viewpoint.

The chief executive was responsible for driving managerial change through the organisation. Such change included reviewing managerial culture, introducing devolved management and empowerment, in addition to developing the performance review system. There was great stress on the integration of these processes:

We need to avoid seeing performance review as a single issue. Performance review has evolved from an entire process of cultural, organisational and managerial change. We have got people to see this as a natural part of organisational and managerial development.

The authority was now much more focused on objectives but were not sure whether this had been brought about by the performance review system, cultural change or the MTP process:

An important message is to do with culture, getting people to think about success and failure in a non punitive sense. We can only achieve change if members are on-board and accept the situation. We need to create a climate where negative reports about departments can lead to a rational discussion at a political level.

Directors were generally supportive of the performance review system (although the impression was gained that non-supporters would be so out of touch with the culture of the organisation that they would not remain in post long).

It was felt that the system had contributed to a corporate management perspective. Bringing together a series of business plans has allowed for the identification of overlap, duplication and lack of clarity and helped the authority to discuss what is really important.

The main strength of the performance review process was seen to be its integration; from organisational goals, MTP to business plans and individual action plans. Its main weaknesses again were seen to be mainly in the political area:

> We have not yet cracked establishing the role of members in reviewing and monitoring policy. Most of our energies have been devoted to getting a robust managerial process in place (i.e. getting our act together). We are good at evaluating new policies but not so effective in evaluating the success of past policies.

Interview with service director

This interview was with the director of social services. The social services department at authority D is very large, employing 7,500 people, with a budget to match.

Policy was developed by the social services committee, but to some extent it was a national policy with a local interpretation. The business planning process and service targets were linked to these policy decisions. It is felt that the performance review process did make an effective contribution to the achievement of departmental goals:

> It is difficult to manage such a large department (7,500 people) and budget. With such responsibilities it is essential that some way is found of ensuring that policies and targets do come right through to the department at the point of delivery. I believe that the review process has contributed to this. In such a large organisation we do not know whether policies are actively translated into service delivery unless we have an effective monitoring system.

Training needs have been quite substantial; performance review requires a degree of discipline which needs to be set off against the culture of social services as a learning profession. Transfer of knowledge of process and performance targets was carried out through the personal action planning process and performance related pay. This officer, however, believed that performance related pay has a downside:

> In that it encourages heavy competition among people who should be working together and avarice; there is a need to be able to reward teams.

This officer also felt that performance review has helped to clarify expectations. This helps to reduce tension between centre and service departments and between service departments and devolved units.

As far as weaknesses were concerned:

> Is it a way to finesse cuts? I have a feeling that sometimes it is. Adjusting targets can be painless internally, although not externally. It is sometimes difficult to strike a balance between top down and bottom up. Its information needs are horrendous. We are developing a much more sophisticated MIS, good management information is particularly important in devolved authorities.

Future development that this officer would like to see is stronger corporate objectives; although the commitment to devolution was very strong, the price is too loose control in the centre. There was a tendency to 'haul in' and check it's OK, but really the system should do that for you.

Interview with member of majority group

The interviewee was chair of the finance, review and information committee and the review sub-group.

This member was a long standing member of the authority and was thus able to outline the history of performance review in authority D. This dated back from local government reorganisation in the mid 1970s. Originally the review process consisted of in-depth audits carried out and written up by members themselves.

The majority group did have a manifesto and responsibility for its implementation rested with a cabinet comprising the group leadership together with committee chairs.

The administration is totally committed to the performance review system; it is part of the culture of the council and essential to its operation. He believes this view is completely shared by members and officers.

The majority group would not be routinely involved in the performance review process unless it exposed major issues. If something damaging emerged from the process it was believed that the opposition would use it. This would not, however, shake the group's attachment to performance review. Conversely, if the review process demonstrated that the majority group were meeting their objectives then this is certainly something that would be used politically.

He was of the opinion that directors of both service and technical departments fully cooperated with the performance review system, since it was completely embedded into the culture of the organisation.

The main strengths of the system were, in his view, that it provided both elected members and officers with the tools required to do their jobs. Perceived weaknesses related mainly to levels of resources available and to the desirability of providing more training.

Overview of performance review at authority D

The most striking feature of the performance review system at authority D was its comprehensiveness and its integration with other systems. There was a full linkage from strategic plan to business plan to personal action plan. In contrast to many other authorities, the system was fully integrated with the budgetary process. A common response from interviewees was not to see the performance review system as a 'stand alone' but to see it as part of a wider management system.

It is also highly significant that performance review appears to be entirely embedded into the culture of the organisation. Unlike authority A, the system was not dependent on the continuing involvement of any one individual for its success. In fact, it is unlikely that an individual who failed to embrace these concepts would be able to operate successfully in this environment. There also appeared to be strong commitment to providing appropriate training.

The system has been developed and enhanced and refined over a number of years to meet the needs of the authority rather than being introduced as a full system at a given point in time.

Nevertheless, a strong feeling persisted that this authority was run on very managerial lines. There seemed to be no strong vision or values underpinning the council's work and a number of respondents cited the lack of involvement of members in the policy/performance review process as a significant weakness of the system.

7 Performance review: general issues

Introduction

In the previous two Chapters we reported on the results of our questionnaire and case study research. In this Chapter we shall try to draw some general lessons and themes from these two studies.

We may also include observation from visits made to other authorities which were not included in the case study chapter because of space restrictions. The scale of performance review work and councils not operating performance review systems has been fully documented in Chapter 5 and will not, therefore, be considered further here.

Types of review system

In Chapter 2 we looked at various schematic performance review schemes proposed by the Audit and Accounts Commissions, Butt and Palmer and Jackson and Palmer.

The overwhelming evidence from both the questionnaire study and the case studies is that little attention is paid to such standard models and that authorities tend to develop their own systems to meet local circumstances. Often the system in use is a modification of an earlier system developed by that authority. Where authorities are influenced externally it is, in fact, usually by a system developed by another authority (Bexley was regularly mentioned).

Interestingly, all the case study authorities developed their performance review systems in this way.

In authority A the approach was to devise a set of corporate goals which cascaded downwards to a set of service goals with associated performance indicators and related targets.

In authority B performance was monitored in two ways: firstly through reviews of specific aspects of service delivery and secondly through the service programmes for departments which reflect the authority's core values and key result areas, relevant targets for these areas and appropriate measures of success.

In authority C the approach was to attach member based performance panels to each committee in order to scrutinise performance.

In authority D the authority had a highly integrated performance review system that had been gradually developed from a more sophisticated system over a number of years. In-depth studies into various parts of the system are still carried out.

The wide variety of approaches and attempts to develop systems to meet local needs illustrates the vitality of the performance review process.

If we now look at the Audit Commission model in more detail, we find that there is little systematic attempt to review performance in terms of costs, resources provided, and outcomes. It may be that this reflects the Audit Commission's view that effectiveness is difficult to measure and the experience of case study authorities suggests that in some cases this is a result of a lack of a clear policy perspective.

There is little evidence to suggest use of the Audit Commission performance monitoring pyramid perspective. In fact in cases A, B and C responsibility for monitoring results is devolved either to departmental or service committee level. In keeping with the Commission's suggestion, targets had been set for indicators but these were generally internally determined rather than based on the Audit Commission's suggested benchmarking figures.

If we compare the case studies with Butt and Palmer's (1985) approach to organising value for money there are a few similarities which suggest that their framework is over ambitious for most councils, particularly in respect of using zero-based budgeting. (Most authorities have problems in linking their budgetary and performance review systems and we shall discuss this later in the chapter.) The two prong performance review mechanism in authorities B and D is in keeping with the distinction drawn by these authors between ongoing review and in-depth reviews of particular service areas.

Jackson and Palmer (1992) suggest that indicators should be related to intermediate and final outcomes and with economy, efficiency and effectiveness. The results of the questionnaire study (see Box F in Chapter 5), indicate that most authorities had considerable difficulties in devising indicators which could be rigidly allocated to one of the above categories. This was also borne out by the case study evidence. Their system also proposes a link with performance related pay; our evidence suggested that this approach is certainly not the norm.

Generally, larger authorities tended to have the most sophisticated systems. This was, however, not invariably the case - various small authorities such as Wyre and Arun had made a substantial contribution to performance review.

Setting up a performance review system

Setting up a performance review system requires an individual or group to initiate the proposal and existence of appropriate circumstances for the authority to adopt it.

It will be remembered that Tables 5.3 and 5.4 contained responses from members and officers about who initiated the proposal to introduce performance review. Not surprisingly, officer responses put more emphasis on their contribution than members and vice versa. In the case study authorities we see examples of a number of different initiatives.

In case study A, the chief executive was very much the driving force, in case study C, consultants initiated the proposal (a rare occurrence according to the results of the written questionnaire) and in case study B it seems that the initial impetus came from members and then was driven through by officers. In case study D the original system was introduced by members but the massive changes and developments to the system which had occurred over the years had been largely officer driven.

Introduction of performance review depends on an appropriate opportunity arising. Questionnaire responses suggest that new systems tend to be introduced when a major internal or external change takes place. The case study evidence tends to support this view. In authority A the introduction of a new chief executive provided the stimulus, in authority B a feeling of crisis and that the authority was losing all sense of strategic direction following years of enforced cutbacks and in authority C the completion of a major consultancy study provided the initiative. Authority D was not subject to such major shocks but the appointment of a new chief executive did result in considerable development and enhancement to the system.

Research shows that the active support of the chief executive is required for the successful introduction of the system. The postal questionnaire revealed that only a handful of chief executives were not supportive of the introduction of performance review and, not surprisingly, these systems were usually unsuccessful.

The Audit Commission believes that the chief executive should be responsible for driving the performance review system. Evidence from the case studies suggests that this, in fact, may not be entirely necessary. In authority A the system was very much driven by the chief executive but the outcome was unsuccessful through failure to gain the ownership of the rest of the organisation. In case study B responsibility for performance review is located with the assistant chief executive and in authority C it is delegated to service departments and members panels. In authority D there appears to be collective responsibility for performance review.

Support from chief officers and members is also essential if the performance review system is to be successful. The questionnaire responses indicated at least some problems with officer support in around 20 per cent of authorities, and problems with member support in around 10 per cent of cases. It could be that these figures may be a little optimistic. In authority A the evidence suggests that most officers were unsupportive. This situation had been brought about by failure to consult and gain their ownership of the system. Members were also rather lukewarm in their support, but given that they had been told that performance review is purely a management tool, this is perhaps not surprising. Authority B's system appeared to attract strong support from both officers and members. Maybe a key lesson here is that the system was introduced in response to strongly perceived need, there was considerable consultation and discretion over the way that departments developed their systems.

In authority C, although officer support appeared satisfactory, the performance review system required a heavy contribution of members' time which created various forms of resistance such as reluctance to join the review panels. In authority D it appeared that performance review was as deeply embedded into the organisational culture that members and officers accepted the system as a matter of course. Here, however, we are considering a system that has been in operation for many years, gradually becoming more comprehensive. Thus, in this authority, we are long past the 'set up' phase of the operation.

The questionnaire study (see Chapter 5, Box A) identifies a number of measures used by authorities to enhance member or officer support for the introduction of the performance review system. These range from joint member/officer informal seminars to rolling programmes of review and discussion sessions. In spite of this, over half of chief executives report genuine difficulties (Table 5.7). Such difficulties were divided into categories: behavioural, technical, resources, political and linkage. As we saw in Chapter 5, the main behavioural problems mentioned have primarily been a lack of support from members and officers and problems with organisational culture. The major technical difficulty has been designing appropriate performance indicators. Training and information management have been the major resources issues. All three of these problems are present in authority A. In case study C, the main difficulty is cooperation with members of the council in the members' panels. At authority D, it was suggested that there were problems in devising the appropriate number of indicators.

The political dimension of performance review

Since performance review should involve questioning whether the key objectives of the council have been achieved, there can be little doubt that it is a political process, and probably in the majority of cases, a party political one. As we mentioned earlier, one majority group leader likened it to the administration 'bearing its soul'.

In authority A, however, it was seen as a purely management tool. In fact one of the politicians in this authority was horrified when a link with the budgeting system was suggested as, in his opinion, this would then make the performance review system 'political'. Authority B had a much more positive view; seeing it as supporting development of a degree of political control following the debilitating effect of years of cuts. The political leadership at authority C believed that it 'should help us as a political group determine clear policies', although it was difficult to get their group to participate. The majority group at authority D felt comfortable in that performance review was a continuing part of their set up. No political group that we interviewed wished to see the end of the system but two opposition groups were very critical of the way that it had been set up and pledged themselves to considerably modify it should they come to power.

The postal questionnaire revealed, perhaps not surprisingly, that opposition groups were typically afforded little involvement in the performance review process, normally limited to having representation on the review committee and this finding was generally borne out by the case study evidence. Majority groups can play a more active role. The questionnaire evidence suggested that their role could vary from highly active 'the majority group sets direction, identifies objectives and decides all actions resulting from review', to having a very passive role. A minority of responses suggested that participation in performance review was confined to key members of the majority party. This limited participation was also identified in case studies A and D.

Although some administrations are concerned that performance review will be used by oppositions to embarrass the majority group, only around 15 per cent of minority groups admitted using performance review for this purpose.

The questionnaire response by majority groups indicated that their political objectives were incorporated into the performance review system in a variety of ways. A common approach is through the targets set or through translating their objectives to a series of key tasks which were then reported upon.

Organisational issues

The questionnaire responses showed that in nearly half the councils performance review was either the responsibility of all committees or service committees only. In around 15 per cent of authorities responsibility was with the policy and resources committee and in roughly the same number responsibility rests with a specific performance review committee. The advantage of carrying out performance review by service committees is that the same bodies who have responsibilities for setting policy and delivery have also the task of reviewing it.

Authority A has a special review sub committee and this is perhaps in line with the very centralised approach taken with this issue in this council. Authority B has a highly delegated structure and this fits in with performance review being delegated to the service level. In authority C, responsibility was taken at the service level but responsibility is in the hands of a panel who are generally not the same members as the service committee. The idea of splitting responsibility for reviewing performance from responsibility for service planning is an interesting one which came from consultants. Lack of interest in participation in the panels, however, perhaps undermined the process. In authority D, strategic responsibility was with the policy and resources committee but service committees were responsible for detailed monitoring of the service implications.

Work on performance review is usually carried out both in the centre (usually as part of the work of policy units) and in the service departments. In authority D, it was estimated that around 50 people were involved in the performance review process in some fashion. Authority A had a dedicated performance review unit. Regrettably, it seemed that this unit was regarded as a 'watchdog' by the rest of the organisation. Possibly, however, the culture of authority A contributed to the above problem.

Performance review systems and their linkages

In the postal questionnaire around 75 per cent of chief executives reported linkages between performance review and their policy planning systems. Slightly fewer leaders reported the existence of such a linkage. Various mechanisms for doing this were reported but service plans appeared to be one of the most widely used approaches. The service plan approach can be very effective. Such plans should give some indication of how the service targets might be achieved. Service planning proved to be an effective way of linking performance to policy in case studies B and D. In authority B, however, the main weakness was the lack of coordination between services. Authority D, however, overcame this problem by employing a medium term plan. In case study A, the link was made by a series of corporate and service objectives. The problem here, however, is that such a series of disembodied objectives gives little idea of exactly how a target might be achieved. Box H of Chapter 5 gives some other mechanisms for potential linkages.

Linkages between the performance review system and the budgetary system are more difficult to achieve. Only about 60 per cent of chief executives believe that such a linkage exists although rather a higher proportion of leaders did so. Box I in Chapter 5 highlighted some responses but it can be seen that many of these are rudimentary.

Some authorities find reallocation of resources particularly difficult when the budgetary situation requires major cuts. Authority B, however, did face up to this problem in eliminating what they regard as 'less essential' activities rather than impose steep cuts across the board. The high level of decentralisation in this authority now makes reallocation between services problematic. As mentioned earlier, members in authority A were horrified by even the thought of greater integration between performance review and the budgetary system. Authority D which had projected the implications of its budget three years ahead had the strongest link with its budgetary system. Although its approach to budgeting is incremental, it attempts to carry out an in depth review of 20 per cent of its base budget each year.

Of the four case study authorities only one formally linked the performance review system to individual staff plans. This was done by authority D's personal action plan which linked individual plans and targets to departmental action plans.

Corporate and development issues

The introduction of a performance review system is likely to present a major change to the way that the authority operates and impacts on corporate culture. Around three quarters of chief executive respondents reported that such an association did indeed exist. As mentioned in Chapter 5 a significant number of answers stress that operating a review system has introduced a greater customer focus on being clearer about what the council's aims actually are.

It could be the case, however, that we face a 'chicken and egg' situation as to whether the introduction of a performance review system leads to a change in corporate culture or, conversely, was a change in the corporate culture a catalyst that led to the introduction of the performance review system?

Perhaps the case study evidence tends to support the latter view. In authority A the performance review system was introduced in an attempt to make the authority more strategic. All the evidence, however, clearly suggests that this approach completely failed to influence the culture of the organisation. Similarly in authority C, the use of member panels involving considerable member participation seemed to have had only a minimal effect on organisational culture.

In authority B, however, development of the system followed dissatisfaction with the council's performance, particularly the perceived gap between policies and performance. Authority D's continuous development of its performance review systems was almost certainly a result of its strong managerial culture.

These results, however, seem intuitively reasonable. It is highly unlikely that an approach or technique will by itself change organisational culture. What an approach such as performance review can do is to give practical effect to a cultural change that has already occurred. Thus, this is quite consistent with the 60+ per cent of respondents who believe that the system has contributed towards achieving a corporate management perspective and attaining corporate goals.

One important finding from this research is that in many cases authorities amend and enhance their performance review systems in the light of experience to help them meet current needs. In Chapter 5, Box L illustrates some of the major changes reported. These range from technical issues such as updating and improving performance indicators to system enhancement such as having better links with policy.

In authorities A and C the performance review system had been introduced only recently which meant there had been little time for changes to be made to the systems. In authority B performance review began as a series of in depth reviews but was then considerably extended by developing the service programmes. In authority D the system again began as a series of in depth reviews carried out by councillors but since that time has undergone major and continuous development.

Evaluation of performance review system

Few chief executives or leaders reported that their performance review system was unsuccessful, although a significant number reported that it was too early to say.

The case study evidence shows a range of views of the success of performance review. In case study A, the chief executive and officer responsible for performance review felt that it was providing clear information and leading to better decisions. All other respondents, however, had serious reservations.

Interviewees at authority B generally agreed that the system had been successful and, in particular, had helped to give strategic direction and restore a sense of purpose that had been undermined by years of cuts. Authority C tended to feel that progress had been disappointingly slow and that the system was limited by members' reluctance to play a full part in the work of the review panels. In authority D performance review was so embedded into the organisational culture that the success of the system was generally taken for granted.

Summing up

From our research we have gained many important insights into practical issues related to the successful implementation of performance review systems. One of these is that, although influenced by the experience of other authorities, Councils generally develop their own performance review systems to meet their own needs and circumstances. This may be threatened by the Citizen's Charter Initiative under which a uniform national set of performance indicators are imposed on local authorities. These questions will be considered in the next chapter.

8   The Citizen's Charter

Background

York City Council was the first local authority to produce a charter for its citizens. York's charter consisted of a broadsheet circulated to the community containing a list of service delivery targets which were linked to the manifesto of the ruling Labour group. There was no strategic or service planning process which helped link the manifesto to these targets.

Nevertheless, these ideas were taken up at national level and all three major political parties have claimed, at one time or another, to be the originators of the charter idea. Thus, Pollitt (1994) observed that:

> Evidently, therefore, the general idea of a charter was one whose political time had come even if the parties disagreed over what its content should be.
> (Pollitt, 1994, p10)

Indeed, the Citizen's Charter became the, then, Conservative government's major initiative for improving the quality of public service. It covers the whole of the public sector including government departments and agencies, local government (including police and emergency services, the NHS and the courts). It also covers key utilities but excludes the rest of the private sector.

The charter begins by laying down a number of principles of public service. According to these principles, every citizen is entitled to expect the following from public services:

1   Explicit standards of service, where possible, backed by target responses or waiting times.
2   Openness about who is delivering a service with most staff wearing name badges.
3   Information about what services are provided, details of targets set and results achieved.

4   Choice, where practicable, using competing providers and by consulting
     with service users.
5   Accessibility with services arranged to suit the convenience of customers
     not staff.
6   Explanation if things go wrong and a well publicised complaints
     procedure.
7   Non discrimination with services available irrespective of race or sex.
     (The Citizen's Charter, 1991)

There is no discussion, however, about why the above principles of public
service were chosen; nor indeed why others were excluded. Nevertheless, we can
see that the emphasis on explicit standards of service, targets and results achieved
must have implications for performance review.

No extra resources are, however, available to meet charter commitments. It is,
we are told:

> About converting the money that can be afforded into even better public
> services.
> (House of Commons Library Research Division, 1992)

Although a document setting out general principles does exist (see Citizen's
Charter above), there is no one Citizen's Charter. The charter system works
through generating specific charters in each public service area. There are now
forty main charters covering all key public services (The Citizen's Charter, Facts
and Figures, 1994a). These range from the jobseeker's charter to the patient's
charter. In some services there are separate charters for England, Scotland and
Wales.

In addition, there are thousands of local charters covering health boards, hospital
trusts etc. A casual perusal of the charters reveal striking differences. For
example, the higher education charter has almost no worthwhile commitment
whereas the one for the railways has significant targets and a compensation
procedure.

The Financial Times of 14 March 1994, p9 provides an interesting comparison
of fifteen different national charters ranging from the then British Rail charter to
the Higher and Further Education charter. This study found that there were
enormous differences in the scope and content of charters. Five charters promise
better services without specific standards (e.g. the higher education charter states
only that applications will be handled fairly and efficiently). Only four charters
were found to have independent checks on whether performance targets are being
met. Where such checks exist they often find standards are not being achieved.
For example, the National Consumers Council found almost 90 per cent of courts
failing to meet standards set. Only three charters have bodies which will take up
users' complaints. Originally charters were drawn up on the basis that standards
should be progressively increased. Over half have not been toughened up. Only

six charters in the audit offer financial compensation for failure to meet the specified standard.

Local authorities and the Citizen's Charter

We will now explore how local authorities fit into the Citizen's Charter process. If the same procedure had been adopted as for the health service, we might have expected that each local authority would be required to produce its own charter (perhaps within an overall framework). Instead, each authority is required to provide specific performance information, usually in the form of performance indicators to the Audit Commission, if the authority is in England and Wales, and to the Accounts Commission if in Scotland. In addition, each authority is required to publish this information in the local newspaper. Authorities do not have discretion about the type of performance information required and nor is there any requirement on them to develop their own Citizen's Charter. In spite of this, however, a number of authorities do publish their own charters.

The Audit and Accounts Commission publish comparative information on local authority performance on a yearly basis. Clearly, this external intervention is likely to influence local authorities' performance review work, and may even take it over if the authority's own system has not been fully embedded.

Progress of the charter

The government has published a number of documents on the progress of the Citizen's Charter. These include the Citizen's Charter report back (1994b), examples of Scottish charters (Scottish Office, 1994) and a comprehensive review, Citizen's Charter 2nd report (1994c).

The latter report announced the existence of thirty-eight charters and tried to claim the credit for improvements in the London underground and health services in England and Wales. Tables are provided on key service achievements and plans provided on further commitments. It also announced a task force to look at and publish details of effective complaints procedures. Also discussed were independent inspections of public sector institutions such as prisons, schools, the probation service, police etc. Although supposedly independent, it should be noted for example that HM chief inspector of prisons is appointed by the government and reports to the home secretary.

Further, there are commitments to establishing regular and direct links between public servants' contributions to the quality of service actually delivered and their rewards and discussion of various performance related pay schemes that can be found in the civil service.

This document, like many other government documents of this time, links delivery of better public services to privatisation and market testing. There is, however, no logically necessary link between these issues and charterism.

A number of independent studies have been carried out into particular aspects of the Citizen's Charter. The government itself commissioned ICM Research (1993) to carry out a consumer survey. This found that 71 per cent of respondents were aware of the Citizen's Charter in general terms. One-third of those questioned, however, had not heard of any specific charter. The highest recognition rate was the patient's charter (40 per cent). Although many felt that the charter could help to raise standards of service, many respondents assessed current standards of public service very favourably, even when compared to the private sector.

A smaller study by Beale and Pollitt (1994) in West London found that the majority had heard of the charter but few could accurately identify a single standard. Other researchers such as McKeown (1993) and Vittles (1993) suggest that quality improvements may have little to do with the charter. Many were already in the pipeline as a result of local initiatives, financial pressure or legislative requirements.

The National Consumer Council (1993) has produced a charter checklist. This proposed that benefits to consumers could be identified by seeing how the charter measures up against a list of criteria. The suggested criteria are:

1   Does the title suggest that the charter covers issues that matter most to consumers and reflect their priorities?

2   Is it possible to comment on the form or content (of the charter) target standards of service and is there an address for making complaints?

3   Does the charter empower consumers e.g. tenant's charter promises consultation?

4   Is there an obligation to inform and be accountable to consumers? This includes readable and user-friendly documentation and information on where to get additional information together with whether there are specific performance standards aimed at the individual consumer.

5   Is there obligation to provide redress - relating to adequate complaints procedures coupled with compensation or other remedies?

Management and the Citizen's Charter

Clearly, implementation of the charter raises a number of management issues. Many of these such as setting targets, empowerment of front-line staff and training issues have already been covered in previous chapters on performance review.

Nevertheless, the charter introduces new managerial problems including the problem that the very existence of the charter may deflect attention from aspects of service that it does not cover.

Local government and the Citizen's Charter

As we have seen earlier, local government was treated rather differently from other parts of the public sector, in that local authorities were required to provide certain types of performance information, rather than develop their own charters. The Local Government Act of 1992 gives the Accounts Commission 'the duty to direct local authorities to public information which will, in the Commission's opinion, assist in making appropriate comparisons by reflection to criteria of cost, economy, efficiency and effectiveness between the standards of performance achieved by different authorities in a financial year'. Similar provisions were made for the Audit Commission or England and Wales.

Although the charter is supposed to take on board the views of users - this does not seem to have taken place. The Accounts Commission Consultation paper (1992c) rather seems to have let the cat out of the bag:

> ... commissioning research to ascertain from a cross section of the population just what they thought were the important factors in determining whether a service was being carried out in a way that met their requirements. It would have to be said that the results of the exercise have shown that public awareness expresses itself in unscientific and imprecise ways which do not lend themselves to prescribing direction in the fashion which would enable inter authority comparison to be made. The result of this is that developments are probably more influenced by the capacity to produce information in numerical form rather than prescribing subjective areas where individual judgements will actually be applied in a real situation to determine satisfaction or otherwise with service delivery.
> (Accounts Commission, 1992c)

Thus, it seems whatever may be claimed afterwards, the process of choosing indicators was dominated by the requirement for numerical information and for comparability.

Accounts Commission citizen charter performance indicators

The first set of performance indicators for financial year 1993-94 was published by the Accounts Commission in 1995. It will be worthwhile making a little effort to review this document.

One of the first points to be taken on board is the claim that the early emphasis on provision of league table information has been dropped:

> In this exercise we are not in the business of providing league tables or making invidious comparisons between authorities.
> (Accounts commission, 1995b, p2)

Instead, it is now claimed that 'the objective is to capture the public's expectation of service through consultation and to measure performance against these benchmarks in order to give sufficient information to enable authorities to learn from each other as to new ways of achieving these objectives in the citizen's interest'.

The report also claims that it will:

1   Help citizens form a view on how their own councils have performed.
2   Provide information that will help each council (its councillors and service managers) and other interested parties to identify those areas where improvements in performance might be possible. Further study will often be required to quantify the precise nature and scope for improvement.
3   Stimulate interest in and debate on, the performance of local government services in Scotland.
     (Accounts Commission, 1995b, p4)

Selecting indicators and collecting information

The Commission claimed that in selecting indicators it had to strike a balance between selecting sufficient indicators to reflect the diversity of council services whilst not overwhelming the reader. In addition, attention was paid to the amount of work involved in collecting the information. The Commission also took into account the fact that some performance information is published in other charters (e.g. school examination results in the parent's charter). In the end, after further consultation, a total of sixty-five indicators were selected.

In the past, comparative information on local authorities has been dogged by data being collected on an inconsistent basis. To try to avoid such inconsistency, the Commission produced a guide which contained definitions for each indicator and described how the information should be compiled.

Suggested information use

It was suggested that a council's performance can be compared in three ways:

1   Standard of performance achieved by the same council in previous years i.e. same council comparison.
2   Comparison of performance of different councils in the same year (providing there is a reasonable similarity between what councils are trying to achieve).
3   National standards - where national standards exist then we can directly compare the extent to which each council has achieved the target. An example of a national standard is that housing benefit applications should be processed within fourteen days.

Legislation requires performance information to be published in the local media. According to Scottish Local Government (1996, p1) there have been almost no enquiries from the public in connection with these adverts.

We shall now review the performance indicators chosen for one service - education (See Table 8.1) which are taken from the report for 1995/6 published in 1997, Accounts Commission (1997).

Table 8.1
Education performance indicators

Pre school experience

1a   The target percentage of primary 1 pupils with experience of pre-school education.
1b   The target percentage of primary 1 pupils with experience of education department pre school education.
1c   The percentage of pupils enrolled in primary 1 with experience of pre-school education.
2   Expenditure per place.

Primary schools

3   Service cost per pupil (including teaching staff), support staff (schools based), education support services (central), administrative support services (central).
4   Expenditure per pupil on individual teaching materials.
5   The percentage of classes, both single year and composite in which the numbers of pupils falls into the following bands:
      15 or less; 16-20; 21-25; 26-30; 31 or more.
6   Occupancy. The percentage of schools where the ratio of pupils to places is: 40% or less; 41-60%; 61- 80%; 81% or more.

Secondary schools

7   Service cost per pupil (including teaching staff, support staff (school based), education support services (central), administrative staff (central).
8   Service cost per pupil on individual teaching materials and equipment.
9   Occupancy. Percentage of schools where the ratio of pupils to places is: 40% or less; 41-60%; 61-80%; 81% or more.

General

10   Assessment of special education needs - average time taken to complete assessment.

11   Repair and maintenance expenditure per square metre of floor area.

The information on each indicator is presented in a particular way. *First,* the indicator is defined. Thus, if we consider indicator (4) *expenditure per pupil on individual teaching material* (primary) this is defined as:

> This indicator shows each council's average expenditure for each primary school pupil on individual teaching materials and equipment such as books, jotters or musical instruments, where these are for use by a single pupil during the relevant period.
> (Accounts Commission, 1997, p14)

This is then followed by a section entitled *points to bear in mind.* Here we find included factors that should be taken into account in interpreting the indicator. For the indicator in question, we have the following points:

1   The extent to which individual schools need to replace outdated and worn out resources.
2   The need for new resources to meet the demands of the new curricula requirements.
     (p14)

(In addition to expenditure on equipment for individual pupils, councils spend substantial amounts on materials and equipment for schools such as video recorders and library books for general use. This expenditure is not taken into account in this indicator.) Indicators are shown in Table 8.1.
A commentary then follows:

> Spending on individual teaching materials varied widely between the 12 councils, within the range of £23-£70 per primary pupil. Seven councils (just over half) spent more than £50 per pupil. Generally speaking, spending was similar to 94/5.

Comments on the education indicators

There are a number of issues which are worthy of comment:

1   Most of the so called indicators are not, on the definition we adopted in Chapter 3, indicators at all. In our view they are *management statistics.* This is particularly the case with various expenditure figures (e.g. expenditure per pupil on individual teaching materials). A reduction in this figure could indicate improved efficiency but it could also indicate a reduction in service. In our view, the only genuine indicators are (1) those

associated with the pre school experience and (9) which is related to the time to carry out the special needs assessment.

That is not to say that costing figures are not of interest. Such information has always been available in the past from the Chartered Institute of Public Finance Accounts (CIPFA), but it was always felt that this information was unreliable. Since great care has been taken to try to get authorities to provide information on a consistent basis, we may perhaps have more faith in the data (though again some figures do look dubious - e.g. £74 per head for expenditure on teaching materials per primary pupil in Dumfries & Galloway compared with £21 per head in Fife in 95/6).

Although such contextual information is very useful for local authorities, it seems not to relate very much to the issues such as defined performance standards etc. associated with the charter.

2   None of the so-called indicators relate to educational outcomes or value added by the education service. Nor in many cases do they seem to relate to clear objectives which might be held by the education service.

3   It may be the case that some of this information is held in the parent's charter but to get a clear impression it is necessary that a comprehensive range of performance indicators should be published together.

4   There is a definite impression that many of the indicators are data driven, there because the information is readily available, rather than being particularly appropriate.

5   The feeling of indicators being unrelated to objectives is reinforced if we look at the indicators related to the housing service. Here we find lots of information about rent arrears, rent losses and response times. Indicators which relate to what might be considered to be the key objectives of a housing service, such as homelessness and warm homes are sadly missing.

Critique of the Citizen's Charter performance indicator approach

There is no doubt that the Accounts Commission has been to a great deal of effort to try to develop a more useful and meaningful process. We have seen, for instance, that there are serious attempts to define the indicator, to identify what points should be borne in mind and to provide an appropriate commentary. Nevertheless, we still have reservations about the entire process. These relate largely to either technical issues or to political and planning issues.

Some of the technical problems have been covered before:

1   We have already mentioned our view that many of the so-called indicators are not indicators at all. This may seem pedantic but we believe there may be dangers in making any piece of quantitative or contextual information into a performance indicator. Some indicators still appear odd and difficult to interpret. For example one indicator is total crimes per hundred police.

This perhaps gives some contextual information about police capacity but is hardly an indicator of police performance.

2   Although presentation of the indicators are hedged around with caveats there is a danger that when comparisons are made this will be ignored. For instance the amount of rent lost due to unoccupied housing in Bearsden & Milngavie in 1994-95 was less than one per cent whereas in Glasgow it was nearly four per cent. In order to make any sense of this comparison it is necessary to have some knowledge of the condition of the housing stock and the proportion of 'hard to let stock' etc.

To quote Page (1980) working in the context of higher education:

> The safest and fairest conclusion is that performance indicators are invaluable, even essential, tools of management information within institutions; they are misleading and unhelpful tools for political analysis between institutions. Unfortunately the latter are more exciting.

3   We have already mentioned in our previous discussions of education and housing of the dangers of performance indicators being data driven. In the author's opinion this problem is encountered throughout the document. We believe that planning perhaps presents the most extreme case. Most would agree that the most important duties of a planning authority is to draw up good quality plans in the light of effective consultation and make good planning decisions. Most of the planning indicators relate to processing time and percentage of population covered by structure and local plans in the last five years. While most would agree that speed of processing is important, this would be secondary to the quality of decisions. By putting all our emphasis on processing times and ignoring quality issues, there must surely be a temptation to sacrifice quality to meet a deadline.

4   We have already mentioned that the charter exercise seems to have had the result of decoupling indicators from their associated policy objectives. Different authorities will, however, because of different local circumstances and different political make-up, adopt different policies. This implies the need for each council to adopt its own range of indicators to cover its own policy perspective. Imposition of a set of central indicators may impose implicit policy objectives on authorities. For example, the implication of the housing indicators would be indicative of a tight control of rent arrears and a rapid turnover of vacant property (but not necessarily a fair letting policy).

Again, all the transportation indicators relate to roads matters and not to public transport. This may implicitly downplay transportation policies based on a heavy public transport emphasis. In fact, the whole area of centrally imposed indicators has resonances within the economic planning system of the former Soviet Union.

We believe that the Accounts Commission document does have value as a statistical compendium about local authorities similar to the CIPFA rating review but the claim that this provides 'performance' information is flawed.

In our view, there is, indeed, a case for communicating performance information to the public. This should be done, however, within the council's own policy context. One way of doing this, of course, would be for each authority to publish its Citizen's Charter. We shall look at examples of the way this has been done in the next section.

Local authority individual Citizen's Charter

We have already mentioned that the idea of the Citizen's Charter was originally derived from York City Council's initiative.

John Sellgreen (1992) describes the development of a charter for Hertfordshire City Council. This development followed a management review in 1990 which was undertaken to produce a more user-oriented and strategic organisation. Following this a survey carried out by MORI found a lack of knowledge of council services and felt that the county council could do more to keep them informed.

The Hertfordshire charter is aimed at:

> Informing the public about the services the county council provides. It is intended to give clear information about services and to state the standard of delivery expected by the public. The charter contains targets for the main services which are delivered directly to customers. Feedback from customers will be important in order to review progress and report back to customers in a year's time.
> (Sellgreen, 1992, p23)

This charter development was the responsibility of senior members from all political groups; it is the responsibility of a steering group of officers to actually deliver the charter. A further feature of the development in Hertford was the opening of a 24 hour hotline and a business charter aimed at business users of the charter.

We shall now look at the types of charter produced by two local authorities.

The Cambridgeshire charter

The Cambridgeshire charter first of all explains who the charter is for:

Our charter sets down standards of service that you can expect and sets out how they will be measured. It makes us responsible to you and it makes sure we regularly check that we are meeting our standards.

The charter process at Cambridgeshire consists of a basic document 'how the council works' and twenty-two subsequent documents on aspects of service. These cover a very wide range of service areas - road building, trading standards, community education, special education needs etc.

The document 'how the council works', for example, gives information on attendance at meetings and how to get appropriate papers, how to contact councillors and officers, and how to get details of council accounts and financial matters. Details are also given of access to council officers and complaints procedures.

We shall now look at one of the individual documents 'obtaining a place in schools and colleges'.

This document confirms the council's responsibility to provide a school place to all children within the 5-16 years age range within a reasonable distance of their home. The council commits itself to produce a guide on getting a place in primary and secondary schools for parents of four year olds and ten year olds respectively and also open evenings where parents can visit schools and ask appropriate questions.

This charter outlines the basis of the allocation of places:

1   Whether your child needs to go to the school for medical reasons.
2   Whether you live in the school's catchment area.
3   Whether your child has a brother or sister at the school.
4   How near you live to the school.

If a child cannot get a place in the school of his or her choice, there is the opportunity of appealing to an independent appeals panel. Once the panel has dealt with all the appeals, the council commits itself to let the parents know by letter within three working days.

Details of the Council's transport policies are also provided. Primary pupils living more than two miles from his or her local school qualify for free travel and the journey time should not be more than forty-five minutes each way.

Similarly, secondary pupils (under sixteen) living more than three miles from their designated local school will qualify for free school transport and the journey time should not be more than seventy-five minutes each way. Similar information is provided about obtaining a place in further education colleges.

If we look at the different charters we find that most of the charters describe the service offered, procedures for obtaining service, complaints procedures and who to contact for further information. Generally, however, with a few exceptions there is little attempt to establish measurable standards of service which is, of course, one of the keystones of the charter's initiative.

The police service is one area, however, where attempts are made to devise appropriate standards of service. For example there is a commitment to answer '999' calls within an average of twelve seconds of the call being passed. Urgent calls should be responded to within an average of ten minutes in urban areas and eighteen minutes in rural areas. Urgent calls are defined as those:

1   Where a life is in danger.
2   Where a serious offence is committed.
3   Where a suspect who is violent or likely to escape is at the scene.
4   Where evidence (including witnesses or identity of an offender) may be lost.
5   Were a person is at risk because of their age, health or some other reason.

Lewisham borough council

Lewisham's Citizen's Charter states that it believes that people in Lewisham have a number of basic rights as citizens. It lists these rights as:

1   Quality services.
2   Fair, just and courteous treatment.
3   To complain.
4   Remedy and redress.
5   Information and consultation.
6   Be heard.
7   A secure and healthy environment.
8   Help in making your views known.

The council is committed to explaining its standards in clear, everyday language, provide clear information about what service standards to expect and what to do if the standards are not met. It also makes information available from information points, libraries and the offices providing services.

Lewisham operationalises its charter through a series of customer contracts. These contracts cover the council's core values, achievement, standards, sources of information, complaints procedures and financial penalties. We shall review these in turn. Lewisham's core values are stated as:

1   Putting services to the public first.
2   Local government serving local communities.
3   Equal opportunities for the people of Lewisham.
4   Being more efficient and effective.
5   Valuing its employees.
6   Aiming for quality.
7   Caring for the environment.

Achievements The service reviewed its achievements during the previous year. These included:

1   Decentralisation by devolving management to fifty service achievement centres.
2   Introduction of additional recycling sites (five extra paper banks) and extra litter bins on the streets.
3   Replaced old public toilets with automatic conveniences at key locations.

The contract establishes a target for Lewisham to become the cleanest borough in Britain.

Many of the contract commitments have appropriate associated standards. For example, on street care the following standards are established:

1   For street lighting *we will*:

Carry out 90 per cent of repairs by the end of the following working day.
Clean and check each lamp once a year.
Change lamps every two years.
Paint lamp standards every five years.

2   On trees along highways *we will*:

Inspect every tree once a year and carry out basic pruning.
Carry out major pruning every five years.
Deal with emergencies either immediately or no longer than six weeks depending on urgency.

3   On drainage *we will*:

Respond to emergency blockages within two and a half hours.
Carry out road gully cleansing on all routes once a year.

For street cleaning in residential areas standards are laid down visually with the use of appropriate photographs. Grade A is a completely clean street which would be expected immediately after street cleaning. Standard B is predominantly free of litter and refuse and would normally be considered acceptable. Standard C is unacceptable with widespread litter and refuse and there is a commitment to restore to grade A within twelve hours.

Grade D is heavily littered and the council commits itself to restoring it to grade A within six hours.

In the *highways* area the following standards are established:

1   Carrying out inspection and survey work once per year.

2   Responding to the following emergency work by the end of the following working day:
Trip hazards in paving greater than 25mm (one inch).
Holes in the road greater than 100mm (four inches).

3   Respond to freezing temperatures within one and a half hours.

4   Carry out the salting of major roads within two hours.

There are also clearly defined procedures for *consultation*. Customer groups have been set up for cleansing services, street care and environmental health and consumers' services.

Complaints procedures are also clearly outlined. If a service has not reached its stated standards, users are asked to ring the local service achievement centre. If not satisfied with the response, then customer services can be contacted.

Lewisham charter also contains an element of *redress*, if services are not delivered to the required standard. For example:

1   If refuse is not collected and the resident telephones before 6pm, then a refund of one pound will be made if the refuse is not collected that day.

2   If the annual planting maintenance on a grave is not carried out, then two years free service will be given.

3   If the service fails to adequately deal with a wasps' nest after two treatments, then the council will refund the cost in full.

In addition, if the service fails to respond to a written complaint within ten working days then the council is committed to send the resident a ten pounds gift voucher.

Thus, it can be seen that Lewisham has most of the main elements of the Citizen's Charter in planning clear service standards that are kept under review, consultation with members of the public, complaints procedures and redress.

Critique of the charter initiative

A number of authors have offered critiques of the charter initiative. These include Pollitt (1994), Deakin (1994) and Prior, Stewart and Walsh (1995). These authors provide critiques of the charter from a number of viewpoints. These can perhaps be best summarised over five different headings:

1   The manner in which the charter standards have evolved. In spite of commitments to give service users more say these have generally been imposed as part of a top down exercise with little participation. In comparing this charter with the People's Charter of 1838 Pollitt states:

> That (the People's Charter) was a document drawn up by the people and presented to the governors. The 1991 version, however, was a document drawn up by the governors and presented to the people.
> (Pollitt, 1994, p12)

In addition, as we have seen earlier the exact status of each standard is not always defined, nor are the consequences of not achieving it clear.

2   There are reservations about the use of incentives such as performance related pay. Apart from possible problems associated with the divisiveness of such a measure in a resource neutral situation, there is a danger that performance related pay will reduce the budget for a service.

3   The question of accountability. Centralisation of development means that accountability is generally associated with the appropriate minister and through him or her to parliament. Given that the impact of local service is felt mainly at local level, this makes accountability very remote.

4   There are various issues about the meaning of citizen and citizenship. To quote Pollitt:

> No general notion of the citizen emerges from the charter documentation. In its place appears to be a *user* or rather *consumer* of public services - and rather a fragmented user at that. The pages of the first two white papers are full of parents, patients, jobseekers and customers, not citizens. To be a consumer is to hold a particular position in a network of market relations. To be a citizen is to be a member of a political community, a richer concept embracing a much wider range of potential relationships.
> (Pollitt, 1994, p12)

Prior et al (1995) also pursue this line of argument. Their main thesis is that the rights of citizens are being recast as rights of individuals with the obligation of government seen as tasks of management. The charter, it is claimed, is based on a concept of the citizen as an individual consumer of public service. No concept of collective rights and little reference to the community can be found in the charter.

These authors feel that instead charters could focus on the community dimensions of citizenship and local authorities' role of providing governance and local leadership as well as services. Such an approach would engage more strongly with the experience and aspirations of the citizenry.

5   Built in political assumption

Virtually all the literature on the Citizen's Charter had a number of political assumptions strongly built in. These involved (Prior et al, 1995):

(i) Competition and market mechanisms will provide choice, ensure quality and value.

(ii) Extending the range of providers will increase choice.

(iii) Accountability is gained not through the political process but through providing information and setting standards.

(iv) Managers respond best to simple payment incentives and market pressures.

There is also little emphasis on the concept of the citizen as the bearer of duties and responsibilities as well as rights.

Pollitt (1994) also claims that the charter bore many marks of its origins as a manifesto item for the 'new right' Conservative government:

> One such is the constant emphasis on 'choice' (i.e. the power of exit rather than voice) and the virtue of privatisation and market testing.
>
> The theoretical citizen cherished by the Conservative government is not a member of any pressure group but rather a heroic lone consumer with time, money and information to back up his or her individual choices. This paragon sounds suspiciously middle class and relatively rare.
>
> (Pollitt, 1994, p11)

The future of the charter

Some of the critiques covered above do have force. In addition, evidence accumulated so far for improvement in quality as a direct result of the charter is equivocal. As we have illustrated earlier, not all management problems have been resolved either. Nevertheless it is unlikely that attempts to establish an effective charter system will simply be abandoned. As Deakin (1994) argues:

> The charter addresses real issues and taps an urge for change that has deep roots. Most public service workers know and have known for a long time that things can and should be done better. Some charter measures trivialise the tasks that need to be undertaken because remedies are often grossly out of scale with problems that poor citizens face. Others are derived from ideology rather than analysis. Some genuine enthusiasm has been misdirected into short term political brokerism. But taking all that away, there is a residue left of potentially important activity which, if set in a different context of sustained belief in the long term future of the public sector, could contribute materially to improving the quality of public service in Britain.
>
> (Deakin, 1994, p57)

The election of the new Labour government may change the emphasis and future direction of charterism. At the time of writing (summer 1997) this still appears to be unclear.

Summary

We have explored the Charter initiative is potential negative implication for performance review in local authorities. We believe that these negative implications are not necessarily the results of the Charter initiative *per se* but the way the Charter initiative has been applied to local authorities. In our view the application of a uniform set of national performance indicators will act as an unhealthy centralising influence on local authorities. This could have been avoided if the approach used for Health Boards (in which each Board developed its own Charter) had been employed in the local government context.

9 The future of performance review

The research evidence

In this chapter we shall consider likely future developments in the performance review area based on both the evidence presented earlier and in light of changes in the political environment.

We may recall the survey evidence which was presented in chapter 5. Chief officers and leaders were asked what future developments they envisaged seeing in the performance review system. Results were presented in Table 5.21. For convenience these results are reproduced below.

Table 5.21
Future developments

Development	Chief officers		Leaders	
	No.	%	No.	%
Linkage	75	46.0	47	31.1
Behaviour/involvement	53	32.5	22	14.6
Technical	24	14.7	66	43.7
Planning processes	6	3.7	5	3.3
Resources	5	3.1	6	4.0
Committee	-	-	5	3.3
TOTAL	**163**	**100.0**	**151**	**100.0**

Boxes M and N in chapter 5 give a selection of typical responses. For example, a typical *response related to linkage* is:

> I would like to link it to the political objectives in the manifesto and use it for strategic financial planning.

An example of a *response linked to behaviour* is:

The identification of a managerial and political consensus around a common purpose.

An example of a *technical issue* is:

Extension of targeting to all major services and developments of measures of consumer satisfaction within service targets.

Example of a *planning issue* is:

Abiding to plan service delivery in the light of agreed priorities and to be able to measure the effects of those priorities.

We shall now turn to the *case study* evidence and the future developments that were mentioned in these cases.

In *Authority A* particular emphasis was placed on behavioural issues. For example the Chief Executive remarked that he wished everyone would see the relevance of performance review and be enthusiastic. The senior manager interviewed was more pointed in his response. He believed that what was needed was complete change of culture, with commitment and enthusiasm from both members and officers. The one issue related to linkage was the need for an effective link with the appraisal system. Linkages with the budgetary system were opposed in principle.

The main behavioural issue mentioned in *Authority B*, was that in future members should be more involved in reviewing the details of service programmes. Future technical developments raised included the need to develop qualitative indicators as well as quantitative ones. Potential future opportunities for looking at best practice outside London were also mentioned. Perhaps the most significant future linkage suggested was a desire to making the planning system more integrated and to introduce a level of planning between mission statement and service plans.

In *Authority C*, a major behavioural change identified was the need to unlock member potential. A director who was interviewed stated that the would like to see better links established with the budgeting system, although it was realised that this might prove to be a 'a long way down the line'.

There was also need for further progress in technical issues such as developing suitable targets and indicators.

A planning issue raised was that in the long run, service committees should review themselves (it will be remembered that this authority used planning panels).

Additional training needs were recognised to ensure consistency of approach.

At *Authority D* a need for further training was also recognised as a problem area. A planning issue raised was the need for stronger corporate objectives with control at the centre being too loose.

Linkages to the budgetary process

In the previous section we saw that one of the most important future developments that respondents wished to see was the establishment of better links with the budgetary process. The research evidence shows that area is generally recognised to be a key weakness of performance review systems. But why do councils find it so difficult to relate their budget to their planning and performance review system?

One reason is that budgets have been originally constructed on a historical basis. Over the years various elements have been added and others subtracted such that it is sometimes claimed that: 'A council's budget is a layer-cake it's past mistakes.'

In other words, the approach to budgeting is incremental with perhaps, therefore, a significant proportion of the budget reflecting post rather than current priorities. Changes that are made from year to year are often made on the basis of a miscellaneous range of 'savings' or 'growth' options which have only tenuous relationships with policy.

Another problem is the practice of constructing budgets annually. The timing of Government announcements concerning Grant-Aided Expenditure and capping limits are decided only three months or so before the latest date for the budget to be declared. The need to reach a capping level means that it is impossible to consider seriously options that might be viable over a longer time-scale. Therefore many sensible strategies for budget reduction are never properly investigated. Such strategies might include:

1   Developing partnerships with other authorities.
2   Developing joint ventures.
3   'Spend to save'.

Instead, options are assessed on their ability to generate savings quickly rather than any policy priority.

We believe that the use of budget 'bids' should be abandoned. In our view the council's link between its policy and the budget is the service plan. If resources are allocated through the service plan the policy implications of increased (or reduced) expenditure should become apparent.

Another useful move to emphasise linkage is the incorporation of the corporate plan and current budget into the same document. This was, in fact, carried out by case study authority D.

The budget process needs to change from a one-off exercise to an all the year process. Also, if an authority were working to a longer term budget, this would greatly improve the opportunity to adopt a more strategic approach. As we shall see later the best value approach suggests such a three year timescale.

It is important to retain community support, particularly in times of difficult budgets and that consultation is carried out with the public. It is essential that

194

such consultation is meaningful and is, therefore, carried out *before* decisions are crystallised.

Best Value

> Councils should not be forced to put their services out to tender but will be required to obtain best value.
> (Labour Party Manifesto, 1997, p34)

As we shall see, the incoming Labour Government's efforts to redeem the above manifesto pledge is likely to make the role of performance review of even greater importance.

The Scottish Office (1997) circular on Best Value (Scottish Office Development Department (SODD), Circular 22/97) recognises what it believes were the positive aspects of CCT. In its view these included clearly specifying service levels, monitoring performance and keeping sound control of payments and costs. This paper also, however, recognises a downside associated with CCT. These disadvantages include the rigidity of tendering, loss of local flexibility, divisiveness and duplication.

Others, of course, also feel that a process that obliged some Council workers, in the main low paid female ones, to have to re-bid for their jobs every few years was totally unacceptable.

In this circular Best Value is described as a process rather than a product. It is described as a search for continuous improvement and puts responsibility for achievement on to the Council, whilst giving them scope for tackling their planning and management in the light of local conditions. Whereas CCT applied only to manual services (although its extension to White Collar services was in the pipeline), Best Value will apply to all services and all employees of the local authority. Rather than adopting a prescriptive approach to best value, the circular proposes certain key principles of the Best Value regime. These principles include.

Accountability

Requiring simple but robust information from across the Council to demonstrate performance.

Transparency

This includes openness, public rights and an effective complaints procedure.

Continuous improvement - a planning framework

Covering the question about what the Council is searching to achieve and also addressing the question of having valid, reliable and appropriately detailed measures of work and cost.

Ownership

Under this principle everyone with an interest/locus should feel some degree of involvement.

Additionally the paper identifies four elements of the system which it claims to be essential

1   Sound governance.
2   Performance measurement and monitoring.
3   Continuous improvement.
4   Long-term planning and budgeting.

Sound governance

This covers the customer/citizen focus, sound strategic, operational and financial management.

The next three issues are also strongly related to issues related to performance review covered in this book.

Performance management and monitoring

According to the Best Value circular, performance information is an essential component of planning, resource control and performance review. The importance of providing the right information at the right time is stressed.

Continuous improvement

This topic covers benchmarking (i.e. comparing performance against other similar authorities). It is suggested that, if standards are best met, then appropriate measures might include testing in open competition.

Long-term planning and budgeting

This relates very much to the issues on linking planning and budgeting which we discussed in the previous section. Here the circular suggests the creation of meaningful budget for three years ahead, developed in tandem with the objectives and targets which the Council has set for itself.

The budgeting exercise must allocate resources which service delivery managers can believe in with some confidence that they will have access to in the forward years.
(Scottish Office, 1997, p10)

Clearly, if this approach is to work then it will be necessary for Central Government to deliver full indication to the Council of the funding available over a three year period and:

A process which allows outlined expenditure and outputs delivered to be measured against budgeted expenditure and targets.
(Scottish Office, 1997)

Clearly, implementation of Best Value cannot be achieved overnight. Three stages are envisaged.

1   *A commitment stage*   In this stage councils have to demonstrate their commitment to working toward Best Value. If this document is unsatisfactory, then CCT will be introduced for that Council. (This document was required by September 1997.)

2   *A progress stage*   A further round of self assessment is proposed for Autumn 1998 to evaluate how far Councils have implemented their compliance plan and what remains to be done.

3   The Government expect that most councils will require a compliance plan which will outline the full implementation of best value by Autumn 1999.

According to the circular:

The ultimate aim must be a self-assessing system, including external validation where a busy Council is demonstrably following and continuously improving Best Value. Best Value means constant change and adjustments to improve. Some would argue that there is nothing particularly new about the Best Value process. They would argue that many of the elements of Best Value, such as reviewing the way that services are delivered, comparing your performance with that of other authorities, simply constitutes good management.
(p13)

In conclusion

We can now see that, whatever their position in the past, all councils will be required to adopt performance review since it is an integral part of Best Value. Furthermore, many other issues that we have discussed in this book, such as linkage between budgeting, planning and performance review systems, will have to be tackled as part of Best Value.

Thus, for the foreseeable future, performance review will be a key feature of all local authority management systems and the work of managers at all levels in the Authority.

It is hoped that the material contained in this book will be invaluable as they come to undertake this task.

Bibliography

Accounts Commission, (1988a), *Narrowing the Gap*, Accounts Commission, Edinburgh.

Accounts Commission, (1988b), *Auditing Guidelines - Value for Money*, Accounts Commission, Edinburgh.

Accounts Commission, (1992a), *Focus on Value for Money*, March, Accounts Commission, Edinburgh.

Accounts Commission, (1992b), *Focus on Value for Money*, November, Accounts Commission, Edinburgh.

Accounts Commission, (1992c), *Citizen's Charter Performance Indicators'*, Accounts Commission, Edinburgh.

Accounts Commission, (1995a), *Local Government Reorganisation and the Stewardship of Public Funds*, Accounts, Commission, Edinburgh.

Accounts Commission, (1995b), *Performance Information for Scottish Councils 1993/94*, Accounts Commission, Edinburgh.

Accounts Commission, (1997), *Performance Information for Scottish Councils 1995/96*, Accounts Commission, Edinburgh.

Alexander, A. (1991), Managing Fragmentation, Democracy and the Future of Local Government, *Local Government Studies* Vol. 17, No. 6.

Audit Commission, (1986), *Performance Review in Local Government: A Handbook for Auditors and Local Authorities: Introduction*, HMSO: London.

Audit Commission, (1988), *Performance Review in Local Government: Action Guide*, London, HMSO.

Audit Commission, (1989), 'Managing Services Effectively - Performance Review', *Management Paper*, No. 5, HMSO, London.

Audit Commission, (1995a), 'Calling the Tune', *Performance Management in Local Government*, HMSO, London.

Audit Commission, (1995b), 'Paying the Piper: People and Pay', *Management in Local Government*, HMSO, London.

Audit Commission, (1995c), 'People, Pay and Performance in Local Government', *A Managerial Handbook*, HMSO, London.

Bains, M. (1972), *The New Local Authorities: Management and Structure*, HMSO: London.

Ball, R. and Monaghan, C. (1993), 'Performance Review: Threats and Opportunities', *Public Policy and Administration*, Vol. 8, No. 8, Winter.

Beale, V. And Pollitt, C. (1994), 'Charters at the Grass Roots. A First Report', *Local Government Studies*, Vol. 20, No. 2, Summer.

Beeton, D. (1998), 'Performance Management: The State of the Art', *Public Money and Management*, Spring/Summer.

Bryman, A. (1988), *Quantity and Quality in Social Research*, Routeledge, London.

Bryson, J. (1988), *Strategic Planning for Public and Non-profit Organisations*, Josey-Bass, London.

Butt, H. and Palmer, P. (1985), *Value for Money in the Public Sector - the Decision-makers Guide*, Basil Blackwell: Oxford.

Carter, N. (1991), 'Learning to Measure Performance: The Use of Indicators in organisations', *Public Administration*, Vol. 69, Spring.

Carter, N. (1994), 'Performance Indicators: Backseat Driver or Hands Off Control', in McKevitt, D. and Lawton, A. (eds), *Public Sector Management*, Sage, London.

Caulfield, I. and Shultz, J. (1989), *Planning for Change: Strategic Planning in Local Government*, Longman, Harlow.

Central Regional Council, (1993), *Service Planning Guide*, Central Regional Council, Stirling.

Citizen's Charter, (1991), *Cmnd 1599*, HMSO, London.

Citizen's Charter, (1994a) *Facts and Figures 'A Report to Mark Four Years of the Citizen's Charter Programme'*, *Cmnd 2970*, HMSO, London.

Citizen's Charter, (1994b) 'Report Back', HMSO, London.

Citizen's Charter, (1994c), '2nd Report', *Cmnd 2520*, HMSO, London.

Clarke, M. and Stewart, J. (1988), *The Enabling Council - Developing and Managing a New Style of Local Government*, LGTB, Luton.

Cuenin, S. (1987), 'The Case of Performance Indicators in Universities. An International Survey', *International Journal of Institutional Management in HE*, Vol. 11, No. 2.

CVCP, (1986), The First Statement by a Joint CVCP/UGC Working Group on Performance Indicators in universities, CVCP/UGC.

Deakin, N. (1994), 'Accentuating the Apostrophe: The Citizen's Charter', *Policy Studies*, Autumn, 1994, Vol. 15 (3).

Denzin, N.K. (1978), 'The Logic of Naturalistic Inquiry' in N.K. Denzin (ed), *Sociological Methods: A Source Book*, McGraw-Hill, New York.

Dochy, F. and Segers, M. (1990), 'Selected Indicators on the Basis of Essential Criteria and Appropriate Assessment Methods for a Quality Assurance System', Paper presented to the CHCPS conference *Quality Assurance in Higher Education* at Utrecht, March 16th, 1990.

Downs, A. (1957), *An Economic Theory of Democracy*, Harper and Row: New York.

Drucker, P. (1973), *Management, Tasks, Responsibilities*, Harper and Row, New York.

Elcock, H., Jordan, G. and Midwinter, A. (1989), *Budgeting in Local Government: Managing the Margins*, Longman, Essex.

Elton, L.B. (1987), 'Warning Signs', *The Times Higher Education Supplement*, 11.09.87.

Financial Times, (1994), 'Major's Public Service Brain Child Fails Test', *Financial Times*, March 14th, 1994, p 9.

Flynn, N. (1993), *Public Sector Management*, Prentice Hall, London.

Hartley, J. (1994), 'Case Studies in Organisational Research' in C. Cassell and G Symonds (eds), *Qualitative Methods in Organisational Research*, Sage, London.

Heseltine, M. (1987), *Where There's a Will*, Hutchison: London.

House of Commons Library Research Division, (1992), 'Ref. Sheet No. 902/8, Economics Affairs, Section', *House of Commons Library Research Division*, June 11th, 1992.

ICM Research, (1993), 'Citizen's Charter customer Survey Research Report', *ICM Research*, London.

IWS, (1983), *IWS Corporate Plan* 1983-9, IWS, London.

Jackson, P. (1988), 'The Management of Performance in the Public Sector', *Public Money and management*, Vol. 13, No. 4.

Jackson, P. and Palmer, B. (1992), *Developing Performance Monitoring in Public Sector Organisations*, University of Leicester, Leicester.

Jones, D. (1995), 'Developing Equality Performance Indicators' in *New Directions and New Partnership*, PPRN, Exeter.

Labour Party Manifesto, (1997), The Labour Party, London.

Layfield (1986), *Report of the Committee of Enquiry into Local Government Finance*, Cmnd 6453, HMSO: London.

Local Government Training Board (1992), *Management of Innovation in Smaller Shire Districts*.

Maud, J.(1967), *Management of Local Government*, MacMillan: Basingstoke.

McKeown, P. (1993), 'Using the Tenant's Charter', Paper presented at Public Administration Committee Annual conference, University of York.

Midwinter, A. and Monaghan, C. (1993), *From Rates to the Poll Tax*, Edinburgh University Press.

National Consumer Council, (1993), *Charter Checklist*, National Consumer Council, London.

Olsen, J.P. (1988), *The Modernisation of Public Administration in the Nordic Countries*, University of Bergen.

Page, C. (1989), 'Management Statistics and Performance Indicators in British Universities'. Paper presented to the 11th Forum of the European Association for Institutional Research, Trier, 29th-30th August.

Paterson, I.V. (1973), *The New Scottish Local Authorities: Organisation and Management Structures* (Report), HMSO: Edinburgh.

Patton, M.Q. (1980), *Qualitative Evaluation Methods*, Sage, Beverly Hills, California.

Perrow, C. (1977), 'The Bureaucratic Paradox: the Efficient Organisation Centralises in Order to Decentralise', *Organisational Dynamics*, Spring 3-14.

Pollitt, C. (1986), 'Beyond the Managerial Model: The Case for Broadening Performance Assessment in Government and the Public Service', *Financial Accountability and Management*, Vol. 2, No. 3, Autumn.

Pollitt, C. (1989), 'Performance Indicators in the Longer Term', *Public Money and Management*, Autumn.

Pollitt, C. (1994), 'The Citizen's Charter: A Preliminary Analysis', *Public Money and Management*, April-June, 1994.

Prior, J., Stewart, J., and Walsh, K. (1995), *Citizenship, Rights, Community and Participation*, Pitman Publishing, London.

Romney, L. Bugen, G. and Micek, S. (1979), 'Assessing Institutional Performance. The Importance of Being Careful', *European Journal of Institutional Management in Higher Education*, Vol. 3, No. 1.

Scottish Local Government, (1996), 'Performance Indicators Round 2', No. 80 Feb.

Scottish Office, (1994), 'Examples of Scottish Charters in Action', *Scottish Office, News Release*, March 16th, 1994.

Scottish Office, (1997), 'Best Value', *SODD Circular*, 22/97, Scottish Office, Edinburgh.

Sellgreen, J, (1992), 'The Hertfordshire Citizen's Charter: A Charter for a Million People', *Local Government Policy Making*, Vol. 19, No. 2.

Smith, Arnold and Bissell, (1991), *Business Strategy and Policy*, Houghton Mifflin Co., Boston, USA.

Smith, J. (1995), *Strategic Management and Planning in the Public Sector*, Longman, Harlow.

Stewart, J. (1990), 'The Role of Councillors in the Management of the Authority', *Local Government Studies*, Vol. 16, No. 4, July/August.

Stewart, J. 'Consideration of Strategic Management in Local Government', Change Again - Conference of PPRN, 1991., PPRN, Norwich.

Stewart, J. And Ranson, S. (1974) 'Management in the Public domain' in McKevitt, D. and Lawton, A. (eds), *Public Sector Management*, Sage Publications, London.

TES (Scotland) (1986) April.

Vittles, P. (1993), 'Beyond the Rhetoric of the Citizen's Charter'. Paper presented at Public Administration Committee Annual Conference, University of York.

Widdicombe, D. (1986), *The Conduct of Local Authority Business*, Cmnd 9797, HMSO, London

Yin, R. (1994), *Case Study Research - Design and Methods*, Sage, London.

Zeithaml, V., Parasuraman, A. and Berry, L. (1990), *Delivering Quality Services - Balancing Customer Perception and Expectation*, Free Press, New York.